MW00466034

THE
HIDDEN
HISTORY
of
DELAWARE
COUNTY

THE
HIDDEN
HISTORY

of

DELAWARE
COUNTY

*Untold Tales from
Cobb's Creek to the Brandywine*

MARK E. DIXON

Charleston — London

THE
History
PRESS

Published by The History Press
Charleston, SC 29403
www.historypress.net

Copyright © 2010 by Mark E. Dixon
All rights reserved

First published 2010

Manufactured in the United States

ISBN 978.1.60949.065.2

Library of Congress Cataloging-in-Publication Data
Dixon, Mark E.
The hidden history of Delaware County : untold tales from Cobb's Creek to the
Brandywine / Mark E. Dixon.
p. cm.
Includes bibliographical references.
ISBN 978-1-60949-065-2
1. Delaware County (Pa.)--History--Anecdotes. 2. Delaware County (Pa.)--History, Local-
-Anecdotes. 3. Delaware County (Pa.)--Biography--Anecdotes. 4. Delaware County (Pa.)--
Social life and customs--Anecdotes. I. Title.

F157.D3D59 2010
974.8'14--dc22

2010038269

Notice: The information in this book is true and complete to the best of our knowledge. It is
offered without guarantee on the part of the author or The History Press. The author and
The History Press disclaim all liability in connection with the use of this book.

All rights reserved. No part of this book may be reproduced or transmitted in any form
whatsoever without prior written permission from the publisher except in the case of brief
quotations embodied in critical articles and reviews.

CONTENTS

CONTENTS

FOREWORD

From the beginning of America, writing "local" history has been the seedbed of nation building. Early "American" writers such as Washington Irving, James Fenimore Cooper and Nathaniel Hawthorne, among others, drew on "local color" tales in finding their own American voice and creating an American literature, and folktales, stories and sacred relics from local places pointed Americans to their own histories devoid of Old World corruptions. At the same time, amateur scientists such as Benjamin Franklin, Thomas Jefferson and James Audubon, among others, recorded, gathered up and even transplanted native flora and fauna on their way to discovering and asserting an American natural history that seemed to promise a brave new world of abundance and possibility. In all this, then as now, locating and discovering one's own place among peoples and a continental expanse so diverse and vast as America has proved essential to any sense of rootedness. A people and a culture ever on the go need to be grounded in something more palpable and real than ideas embedded in parchment promises such as the Declaration of Independence and the Constitution. They need connections to particular places and pasts to create any sense of community. Enter local history.

For a century or more from the beginning of the republic, local history writing was almost wholly the province of the "amateur," who collected the artifacts, tales and documents for display and description. The works they produced were antiquarian rather than analytical, but they were also unashamedly promotional in celebrating a past of progress and the virtues of a particular place and people. By the late nineteenth century, with the emergence of history as a profession ruled by new standards of "objectivity" and scientific method, local history writing moved, in part, into the hands of scholars supposedly taking a more critical assessment of the character and conduct of different people in different places, often within a comparative framework that showed both the uniqueness and sameness of American places. Local history also bloomed in the publication of numerous county histories that were encyclopedic in coverage and in illustrated histories gathering up postcards, photographs and other images to make "real" places and people no longer standing or alive. All the while, local historians published books, booklets and articles in magazines and newspapers that highlighted an event, building or personality worth remembering, often reverentially. Local history writing gained new interest and a wider audience with the rise of the "new social history" from the 1960s on, in which historians shifted primacy from studying kings and queens to looking at the daily lives of the common sort, and others, and found new purpose in the genealogical records, oral histories, folklore, architecture and anything left by people that revealed who they were, what they believed and why they behaved as they did. New interests invited new looks at the past, as women, immigrant and ethnic groups, minorities and others previously left out of the national narrative now entered the field of vision of local history and the "new social history." Then, too, the very mobility and instability of America, moving faster each decade, quickened interest in local history. Whether in an airline magazine, newspaper or any of the many local or regional magazines promoting culture, consumption and community awareness, local history now commands an ever-expanding audience. It also seems to affirm the old saw that all history is local history.

Mark Dixon's new book on Delaware County, Pennsylvania, and its environs exemplifies the best traditions of the genre of local history writing. It does so not only by discovering and recovering a cast of personalities significant in their own time but also by connecting them to the larger economic, social and cultural development of the region and the nation. Delaware County officials and historians take pride in noting that the smallest county in the commonwealth has one of its biggest histories. It was the site of the first European settlement in what became Pennsylvania; the landing point for William Penn as he set about creating his "Holy Experiment"; the place where the first English Pennsylvania government met and laid out the colony's laws that included protections for basic civil liberties; and a battleground during the American Revolutionary War. Much of the writing about Delaware County stops there, as if the colonial and Revolutionary eras explain all and as if the only trajectory for the county, the commonwealth and the country was "freedom" growing ever larger and stronger. As the seedling sprouts, so grows the tree—that is the assumption and implication of most accounts. Not so for Mark Dixon. He extends the time frame from colonial beginnings to the present day. More important, he moves beyond the traditional boundaries of county history (and histories) by showing how place and people intersected, often in contradictory ways. And he maps lives and histories in which the arc of freedom is not so sure and one-directional.

Saints and scoundrels, the innocent and damned and a full array of people, from those wearing silk stockings to those having no shoes at all, people Dixon's world. Whatever their character and conduct, they are very much a people in motion. Many are on the make, and some are on the take. Some are trying to remake themselves and the world. The county's location between North and South in many ways and on the borderlands of modernizing America opened it to new possibilities. It was, for example, a pathway to freedom for fugitive slaves running from neighboring slave states, just as it laid out the pathway to conscience and social justice commitment for Martin Luther King Jr. when he studied at Crozer Seminary in Chester. It was a place of innovations and inventions, including the creation of the uniform universal screw that literally liberated construction from the vagaries of imperfect and diverse fasteners.

But Dixon's Delaware County also turns on paradoxes of "freedom" and "success" for some coming from the "unfreedom" and "failures" of others, whether imagined or real. Thus, for example, women pushing for the vote as the means to redeem politics and save democracy met up against women who feared that gaining the ballot was a devil's bargain that would corrupt family and undo the republic. And thus, too, the Baldwin Locomotive Works, at one time the largest company in America and the principal manufacturer of railroad engines, left Philadelphia to set up shop in Delaware County, where it might be "free" from labor organizers in the city. Ironically, the company's move did not save it from collapse as the automobile, truck and airplane moved America off the rails and caused many manufacturing jobs to leave the county. Earlier, moving water in the county's many streams had powered the paper, grist and flour, spinning and textile and other mills that made the Delaware Valley a "workplace for the world," and access to the Delaware River linked county producers with world markets and brought in new people, products and ideas. Tall masts in harbors competed with church steeples in town squares to mark the way(s) people found and followed their interests. A century later, oil refineries fouled the air, while nature lovers lobbied governments to set aside land for parks and preservation and placed easements on private lands to keep them from some future despoilation. Delaware County shipyards built the great fleets that helped win the war against fascism and for the Four Freedoms Roosevelt had enunciated in the Atlantic Charter, but the Cold War that came after the hot war did not need the shipyards so much. They floundered and failed, and prosperity yielded to poverty for many workers. As industrial jobs went elsewhere, the county was left with what became the poorest city in the state; it sits not far from some of the wealthiest homes of the DuPonts and their heirs and others whose forebears had made their fortunes in the world of brass-knuckled capitalism. Defense spending still counted for much, in making helicopters for example, and the county that once led the way in private initiative and enterprise grew dependent on public money for its work, transportation and even entertainment.

Through all this, Dixon's sure hand takes the reader to the people making and unmaking this complex place. He keeps the history on course. Dixon thus succeeds in giving us a people's history in both senses of the term. It is at once a history focusing on particular people whose lives illume worlds larger than the homeplace, and a history written from the perspectives of the many and diverse people in or coming through the county and its environs. As such, it is local history that knows no bounds.

Randall M. Miller
Saint Joseph's University

ACKNOWLEDGEMENTS

My view of history was shaped disproportionately by Corinne Robinson (1904–1993), who taught my eleventh-grade American history class at East Grand Rapids (Michigan) High School in 1967–68. For years, I have remembered "Mrs. Robinson"—I didn't know her first name in those days— as seeming almost personally offended by U.S. actions in the Mexican War. But that may not be true. After comparing memories with former classmates, what I recalled as anger may instead have been her teaching method.

Mrs. Robinson gave us context for each history fact. Rather than simply tell us that something happened—and expect us to remember it—she emphasized who made it happen, what he (or she) got out of it and the consequences for others.

In the case of the Mexican War, we learned that a major result of the conflict was to open Texas to slavery, something previously forbidden by the Mexican government. We learned that Henry David Thoreau chose to be jailed rather than pay a tax to support this. And we learned that Abraham Lincoln, then in Congress, challenged President James K. Polk's claim that the cause of the war was an attack on U.S. troops by Mexican forces. (Lincoln, suspecting that the Polk administration was attempting to pass off a fabricated Tonkin Gulf-style "incident," demanded that it "show me the spot" where the attack had occurred.) Now, I suspect that Mrs. Robinson merely gave us information to chew on, and I chose to be outraged.

Not everyone gets teachers like this. My high school friend Steve had a history teacher he remembers as "dull as gray sky." Another, Linda, spent the year with a member of the Greatest Generation who, she remembered, "glossed over everything before and after World War II" and attributed every turning in U.S. history to the influence of "rugged individualism."

In these stories, I've tried to make room for human nature, which is history's only real constant. Circumstances change, but people rarely do. So, history can turn on greed or altruism, lust for power or humility, vengeance or forbearance. Such stories are necessarily complex, so you'll rarely find them in textbooks or on monuments.

Wherever she is, I hope that Mrs. Robinson would approve.

1688: A Parable of Preemptive War

War has few risks for politicians as long as they win. If they warn of danger and are correct, politicians who start wars will be heroes. If they're wrong but the wars are won anyway, they'll still be heroes.

Which proves that Caleb Pusey (1651–1727) was a poor politician. In 1688, Pusey—a miller, business partner of William Penn and, later, a justice on colonial Pennsylvania's supreme court—heard panicked warnings of an imminent attack by the Delaware Indians. But rather than rally troops, Pusey went unarmed to the Indian camp. What he found was the Indians going peacefully about their business. And after a brief but not unpleasant visit with a bemused tribal chief, Pusey went home.

There was no war—indeed, no *reason* for war.

"A more heroic figure than blustering Myles Standish" is how early Pennsylvania historian Robert Proud described Pusey. Standish, who arrived on the *Mayflower*, favored preemptive attacks to deal with the Pilgrims' Indian neighbors. In 1623, at Wessagusset, Standish lured several chiefs to a feast and then killed them—stabbing one himself—and put the leader's head on a pike at the Plimoth colony. So, naturally, Standish is memorialized in Massachusetts with a 116-foot granite monument; Pusey, only by his house—thought to be the oldest in Pennsylvania—on Race Street in Upland.

That's typical. Americans understand history primarily as stories of conflict in which heroes save the day. Heroes help us define who we are and what we believe. For many of us, a mundane suburban life might be unbearable without the sense that, under the right circumstances, we could be heroes, too.

When word came to Caleb Pusey's house in Chester—now thought to be the oldest house in Pennsylvania—that local Delaware Indians were planning to massacre the European settlers, Pusey went unarmed to the Indian camp to investigate. *Courtesy of Library of Congress.*

Pusey, however, seems to have been content to remain a miller. Born into a Baptist family with nine children, Pusey was raised in the village of Upper Lambourn in Berkshire, England. His father, William, was a malt miller, but Caleb was a maker of lasts, the wooden forms on which leather shoes were made.

Sometime in the 1670s, Pusey joined the Quakers. Why is not known. Both groups were considered radical, but the Quakers slightly more so, which may have appealed to Pusey's youthful idealism. After writing his first Quaker religious tract in 1675, he moved into the inner circle of William Penn, himself a prolific writer.

Four years before receiving his huge land grant in America, Penn had toured Germany and Holland, where he preached and made the contacts that later brought crowds of Dutch and German immigrants to Pennsylvania. But the many mills turning along the Rhine and its tributaries also impressed him. When the time came to settle his own colony, Penn turned to the miller's son—Pusey—to see that Pennsylvania had a mill, too.

Constructed in England, the inner works of Penn's mill arrived aboard the *Welcome* with Penn and were assembled the following year on Chester Creek. Penn himself attended the laying of the cornerstone. A joint stock company owned the enterprise, with Pusey acting as miller and resident agent.

It was tough work. The mill was washed away and rebuilt several times. Then, Thomas Coebourne defied the Chester Mill's supposed monopoly and built a competing mill in Middletown Township. Pusey sued on behalf of his partners but lost—and numerous mills soon went up on other area creeks. Despite this, the Chester Mill prospered, and Pusey eventually came to own it in his own right. The structure no longer stands, though its weather vane is preserved at the Historical Society of Pennsylvania.

Pusey was also busy elsewhere. For eleven years, he was a member of the Provincial Assembly and of the Governor's Council, a board of advisers akin to a presidential cabinet. He frequently served on juries, was appraiser of estates, collector of taxes, one of two justices of the peace for Chester County and sheriff and supervisor of Penn Charter Academy. Pusey was a signer of Penn's 1701 Charter of Privileges and, in addition, a member of the committee that measured the boundary between Pennsylvania and Maryland. (His estate included surveying tools.)

Pusey also appears to have been fully committed to the Quaker vision of a peaceful New Jerusalem in the wilderness. In the future, Quakers would yield to political pressure to support various colonial wars. But in the colony's infancy, they succeeded in keeping Pennsylvania both unarmed and without need for arms.

Managing foreign policy without an army requires extraordinary diplomatic skill. So it is significant that Pusey, from his arrival until his death forty-five years later, was nearly always among those who dealt with the Indians. As late as 1721, when he was seventy, he served on a delegation sent to soothe the feelings of the Five Nations at Conestoga. There, the Mingo interpreter Ghefaont complained of white traders calling their young men "dogs." It was a problem that seems to have been rooted in the sale of rum to the Indians, which Pusey's delegation promised it would try to restrict.

On other occasions, Pusey was simply fierce. In the 1690s, when George Keith led a schism within the Quakers, Pusey produced a torrent of pamphlets refuting Keith's assertion that the Friends were insufficiently Christian. His titles included *George Keith once more brought to the Test, and proved a Prevaricator*; *The Bomb searched and found stuff'd with False Ingredients*; and *A Modest Account from Pennsylvania of the Principal Differences in Point of Doctrine between George Keith and those of the People called Quakers*. In the latter, Pusey took on the conservative Keith's idea that salvation depended on knowledge of Christ's death and suffering.

"This I deny," wrote Pusey. "Even as many have suffered hurt through the disobedience of the first man, Adam, who have not known expressly that ever such a man was, nor the manner of his disobedience; so even why may not many receive benefit through the obedience of Christ...who have not known expressly his coming and sufferings?"

Caleb Pusey was a big guy. No portrait exists, but Penn once sent his friends some broad-brimmed hats—the kind he wears on the Quaker Oats box—as gifts. Only the largest fit Pusey.

This, then, was the man who, "in or about the year 1688," heard a report that five hundred Indians were assembling at Brandywine Creek in preparation to kill all the English settlers. According to Proud's 1798 history of Pennsylvania, the story originated with two Indian women in New Jersey who repeated it to "an old Dutch inhabitant" near Chester, with the added warning that the attack would come on the following Wednesday. According to Proud, who based much of his history on papers left by Pusey, Quaker leaders labeled the story a rumor. But at 10 p.m. on Wednesday, a messenger arrived at Chester, shouting that three families were surrounded by the Indians. Investigators found three empty houses but no bodies and no signs of murder. "Their inhabitants, alarmed [by the rumors], had fled," wrote Proud.

Hysterical reports soon reached the governor's council at Philadelphia. One of the members, "supposed to be Caleb Pusey," wrote Proud, volunteered to go to the place, provided five others would ride along. There is a problem with Proud's account: Pusey was not a member of the council in 1688. He was, of course, well known to council members and may even have been present at their meeting. In any case, the men soon rode out toward the Lenape town, located on the east bank of the Brandywine off present-day Rocky Hill Road, in a neck of land formed by a bend of the creek.

"Instead of meeting with 500 warriors," reported Proud, "they found the old king quietly lying with his lame foot along the ground and his head at ease on a kind of pillow, the women at work in the field and the children playing together. When they had entered the wigwam, the king presently asked them very mildly, 'What they all came for?'"

The whites repeated the story and asked what grievances, if any, the Indians had against the English. Not a one, said the chief, who added, "'Tis true there are about 15 pounds yet behind of our pay for the land which William Penn bought. But as you are still on it and improving it to your own use, we are not in haste for our pay. But when the English come to settle it, we expect to be paid." The chief was assured that the tribe would be paid.

Then one of the Quakers—Pusey perhaps—felt the need to make a speech, saying "that the great God who made the world," by causing the rain and dews to fall on the lands of both the Indians and the English, thereby proved that He loved both equally, "so they were mutually bound to love one another." Actually, the Quaker said a lot more, and one might imagine the old chief's eyes rolling at the extended yadda-yadda.

"The king answered," wrote Proud, "'What they had said was true; and as God has given you corn, I would advise you to get it in (it being then harvest time) for we intend you no harm.'"

There have been different spins on the story. A version published in the *Philadelphia Press* in the 1920s reported that Pusey "mediated" for peace—suggesting that an attack might have actually been planned. In 1955, local historian Charles Heathcote wrote in a Kennett Square newspaper that the Lenape, enraged at having been swindled of their furs, really were prepared to attack.

"When Pusey learned of this proposed attack," wrote Heathcote, "he met the chiefs of the band and demanded that they should depart from the county and he promised them that they would receive justice." The Indians, admiring his courage, complied.

None of these stories is well documented. Neither the chief nor any of Pusey's companions—if Pusey was even there—are named. The date is fuzzy. And there's the main question: Was the attack averted by persuasion? By demand? Was an attack ever planned at all? Would a preemptive attack by the English have been appropriate?

Believe what you will. We all do. History is less about what happened than it is a conversation about the sort of leaders we want to follow and the people we want to be.

1715: God's Footstool

S ometimes a crime is just a crime. Sometimes it's an opportunity. Convicted in 1873 of voting illegally, Susan B. Anthony used the incident to promote women's suffrage. In 1925, modernists used John Scopes's conviction for teaching evolution to ridicule Christian conservatives. In the 1950s, Richard Nixon used his role in the perjury conviction of former communist Alger Hiss to build a political career.

Locally, in 1715, opponents of Pennsylvania's Quaker government used the murder of Jonathan Hayes—a Marple farmer and justice of the peace—in an attempt to seize control of the province. The Quakers fought back (literally) with blood: rather than scrap their "Holy Experiment," they scrapped what their critics called a soft-on-crime legal code.

"The 'Great Law' of 1682, passed under...William Penn and his immediate friends, reduced the death penalty to cases of treason and murder," wrote historian Isaac Sharpless. "This stood until 1718." Then, in a deal to retain power, the Quakers passed a new act that extended the death penalty to robbery, burglary, malicious maiming, arson, manslaughter by stabbing and counterfeiting.

Little is known of the murder itself. A biographical sketch of Hayes's father, Jonathan Sr., who served in the colonial assembly in 1689 and 1697, reports that the son was killed "while attempting to break up a quarrel." The killers' final appeal, submitted just before they went to the gallows in 1718, asserted that "they never had the least design or intention of killing."

The killing—in March or April 1715—was the first recorded murder in Chester County. Genealogical data on the Hayes family indicates that Hayes

Vice President John Nance Garner (right) didn't consider the swearing-in of two new senators in 1936 a sufficiently momentous occasion to even put down his cigar. In colonial Pennsylvania, however, oath-taking was passionately debated and the subject of tough political dickering. *Courtesy of Library of Congress.*

died in Marple Township, which, therefore, was probably also the scene of the crime. (Marple became part of Delaware County in 1789.)

Born in Cheshire in northwest England, Hayes arrived in Pennsylvania with his parents aboard the *Friendship* in November 1683. The elder Hayes seems to have been arrested in England the previous June for attending Quaker meetings and released only upon his promise to go to Pennsylvania. When they left, the Hayes family took two thousand pounds of various goods—including window glass and pewter—for resale. That sort of shrewdness enabled Jonathan Sr. to accumulate enough money to purchase more than three thousand acres of land by the time of his death in 1712. This acreage included six hundred acres in Marple, adjacent to the property of another settler, John Pugh, who operated a mill on Darby Creek. After the senior Hayes's death, his property passed to Jonathan Jr.

The killers—Hugh Pugh, a millwright possibly related to Hayes's neighbor, and Lazarus Thomas, a laborer—were captured almost immediately and jailed at Chester. The court's first move was to assign three justices to find a place "more convenient" than Chester for a trial. The murder had caused a sensation in the county. Hayes's Marple neighbors wanted the trial conducted locally.

Then things got strange. Local justices of the peace refused to take evidence from witnesses. Justices of the Pennsylvania Supreme Court, which tried all capital cases, declined to proceed. Ultimately, Pugh and Thomas were released on bail.

At issue was the Quakers' legal right to use an affirmation rather than an oath to give evidence or be a juror. The difference—simply promising to tell the truth (an affirmation) versus similar language with the words "by God" attached (an oath)—seems arcane. But the issue was grist for an early culture war in the same way that liberals and conservatives today occasionally squabble over use of the Pledge of Allegiance and Ten Commandments.

Most witnesses and potential jurors were Quakers, who based their refusal to take oaths on a literal understanding of Christ's admonition against the practice in the Sermon on the Mount:

> *But I say unto you, swear not at all; neither by heaven, for it is the throne of God; nor by the earth, for it is the footstool of his feet; nor by Jerusalem, for it is the city of the great King. Neither shalt thou swear by thy head, for thou canst not make one hair white or black. But let your speech be, Yea, yea; Nay, nay: and whatsoever is more than these is of the evil one. (Matthew 5:34–37)*

Very few Christian churches have taken Christ's prohibition literally, in part because oaths seem to be approved elsewhere in Scripture. Quaker critics noted, for instance, that Paul of Tarsus is recorded—without criticism—swearing oaths. To which the early Quakers responded: perhaps, but we follow Christ, not Paul of Tarsus.

Then, too, the Anglican, Puritan and Catholic churches had—or, at least, had the memory of—controlling governments. In England, the Anglicans comprised the state church. So they tended to be more understanding of secular officials' desire for tools to control the population. Quakers, in contrast, remembered what it had been like to be the targets of a hostile government.

In England, the establishment found the Quaker position useful. When one wanted to put a Quaker in jail, all one had to do was demand that he swear an oath of allegiance to the Crown. Refusal was a crime, so the tactic worked nearly every time.

In 1668, Quaker founder George Fox told of an English Quaker who was robbed of his livestock and appeared before the local court to press charges. Tipped that the man was a Quaker, the judge demanded that he take the oaths of Allegiance and Supremacy, recognizing the king. "So, they cast the Friend into prison," said Fox, "and…let the thief go at liberty that had stolen his goods."

Quakers' refusal to take oaths or remove their hats before a magistrate and their insistence on holding banned religious meetings in public led to six thousand Quakers being imprisoned between 1662 and 1670. But a couple of centuries later, their reputation for honesty would lead entrepreneurs to slap the name "Quaker" on everything from motor oil to breakfast cereal.

The founding of Pennsylvania, however, put Quakers in nominal charge of a government—"nominal" because, although most of the population and Penn himself were Quakers, English law nevertheless required that all officeholders take an oath of allegiance to the Crown. Penn got around this by appointing Anglicans whom he thought he could trust to manage the colony. He never served as governor himself.

In 1700, and again in 1705, the Pennsylvania Assembly passed legislation allowing an affirmation not mentioning God for all purposes. Both times, after fierce complaints from Anglicans in England and Pennsylvania, the home government revoked the acts as too liberal.

In 1710, the Pennsylvania Assembly passed a third law allowing the so-called Pennsylvania Affirmation and warning of "a failure of justice if so considerable a number of the inhabitants" were "incapable of giving evidence." As the colony awaited official reaction from London, Pennsylvania courts stopped functioning. Many Anglican justices of the peace refused to act because of their doubts about the affirmation's legality.

The affirmation was not London's only gripe. The English establishment also disliked Pennsylvania's lenient legal code. In England, death was prescribed for more than two hundred offenses, ranging from rape and arson to shoplifting and the malicious maiming of cattle.

The assembly learned in 1712 that its 1710 affirmation had again been overturned. After three strikes, Quaker politicians realized they must cut a deal. A new statute gave individuals "free liberty" to choose an oath or the English affirmation. Some Anglicans had complained that their "right" to take an oath had been infringed by Quaker justices who refused to administer it.

Still not good enough. London repealed this act, too. In England, the Earl of Clarendon complained acidly that Pennsylvania's Quaker legislators were "little better than rebels."

After several years of wrangling, colonial Governor Charles Gookin (an Anglican) decided that Quaker legislators needed a scare. During the 1716 assembly—with Pugh and Thomas at liberty and continuing to shock Chester County with their "publick Rioting, Caballing and fighting"—Gookin announced that a 1715 parliamentary statute extending the English "by God" affirmation to the colonies also carried its restrictions. Therefore, Quakers could not vote, hold office, testify or serve on juries.

Legislators vehemently disagreed but realized that something had to go. While most Friends would refuse to swear "by" God, the leaders came to realize that most could tolerate an affirmation made "in the presence of God." After all, wasn't it merely stating the obvious? That we are always in God's presence?

To sweeten the deal, the Quakers enlarged the death penalty. David Lloyd, speaker of the assembly, wrote *An Act for the Advancement of Justice*, which added such offenses as burglary, arson, witchcraft and sodomy to the list of capital crimes. To enforce this, the act accepted affirmations with the "in the presence of" language.

It was a win-win-win. London got the more severe criminal code it wanted. Anglicans got their God-talk. And Quakers maintained their control of the colony without violating their religious beliefs—at least, not too much.

The act was passed, and in early 1718, Pugh and Thomas—who, amazingly, had not fled—were retrieved, tried and condemned in a trial at Chester attended by the new governor, William Keith. On May 17, Keith and his council considered the killers' final appeal, which complained that "17 of the Grand Inquest who found the Bill of Indictment…and eight of the petty Jury who found them Guilty were Quakers…and were qualified no otherwise than by an affirmation."

But that obstacle had been removed. Keith declared that the trial had been "most favourable and fair…and the proofs were so pregnant, and the crime so black, as most justly did infer the punishment of death to be inflicted on the guilty persons."

Pugh and Thomas were hanged the next day.

In 1725, the assembly passed legislation allowing the Quakers' godless affirmation, which the Crown approved after local Anglicans conceded that society had not collapsed under Quaker rule.

As a result, today's officeholders—even presidents of the United States—can choose for themselves whether to swear or affirm when they begin their terms of office. Presidents, though, have overwhelmingly been the sorts of guys who have chosen to swear. (Only John Tyler, Franklin Pierce and Herbert Hoover, a Quaker, chose to affirm.) Of those who chose to swear, all have followed the lead of George Washington, who, at his 1789 inaugural, added the words "so help me God" (not required by the Constitution) while laying his hand on the Bible (also not required) that forbids oaths.

And so everyone got what they wanted—except Jonathan Hayes, Hugh Pugh and Lazarus Thomas.

1778: Standing on Sandy's Shoulders

A hanging kills but, officially, isn't vindictive. The goal is to finish the job, nothing more. Drop, snap, done. But sometimes the powers that be can't resist savoring an execution. When former Iraqi dictator Saddam Hussein was hanged in 2006, for instance, witnesses couldn't resist ridiculing him on the scaffold and then dancing around his corpse.

Americans are not incapable of such thoughts. During the Revolution, James Fitzpatrick (1748–1778) was executed at Chester in a hanging so unpleasant it may have been deliberate. Fitzpatrick, an American deserter, had gone over to the enemy. Later, he specialized in robbing Patriot officials while humiliating those trying to capture him. Some accounts have accused Fitzpatrick of giving the British information that helped them win the Battle of the Brandywine, but he was never formally accused of that, much less convicted. And Fitzpatrick himself never killed or permanently harmed anyone.

Meanwhile, the Founding Uncles who ran Revolutionary Pennsylvania weren't above using their authority against those they hated. They hated Fitzpatrick.

Born in West Marlborough to a Scots-Irish father and a Quaker mother, Fitzpatrick is best remembered as "Sandy Flash," the nickname used in stories by writer Bayard Taylor. Taylor changed most names, but Sandy Flash is one to which Fitzpatrick might actually have answered. According to a 1940 article in the *Kennett News & Advertiser*, he was occasionally seen galloping home from parties in the early dawn with his long, red hair streaming—as a local farmer described it—"like a sandy flash."

The original Chester County Courthouse—built in 1728 and still standing on the Avenue of the States in Chester—was the scene of the 1778 trial of James "Sandy Flash" Fitzpatrick, who was subsequently executed in a (deliberately?) botched hanging. *Courtesy of Delawarecountyhistory.com.*

Fitzpatrick's father disappeared when he was young. In 1762, at age fourteen, he was apprenticed to John Passmore, on whose Doe Run farm he lived in a two-story tenant house with his mother. When the apprenticeship expired on Fitzpatrick's twenty-first birthday, he was six feet, four inches, blue eyed and, according to one source, "a very Hercules in build and an Apollo in looks." Now a skilled blacksmith himself, he worked at several Chester County forges.

In the spring of 1776, Fitzpatrick joined the Pennsylvania Flying Camp, a militia unit organized to reinforce the small Continental army. No militia were drafted before 1777, so Fitzpatrick enlisted voluntarily. Chester County contributed a two-thousand-man battalion, which marched to New York in July with Fitzpatrick in the ranks.

In August, Fitzpatrick participated in the Battle of Long Island, a poorly planned battle in which George Washington tried to push the British under General Sir William Howe out of New York—and was instead pushed out himself. Fitzpatrick was wounded and, soon after, deserted.

It wasn't the war; it was the officers.

"Never subordinate in the best of times, [Fitzpatrick] refused to perform some menial (and perhaps demeaning) task assigned to him by a superior in camp," wrote historian Phil Magitti. "As a consequence, Fitzpatrick, not fully recovered from his wound, was…flogged for insubordination." This was an era in which each officer was entitled to one soldier—or slave, if he owned one—to use as a personal servant. Possibly, Fitzpatrick had told the man to polish his own damn boots.

He swam the Hudson at his first opportunity and reached Philadelphia, where he was recognized and imprisoned until he promised to return to the ranks. He promptly deserted again. The following summer, Fitzpatrick was mowing hay in Passmore's field when two Continental soldiers appeared to arrest him. Until that moment, his desertions might still have been forgiven; the army needed men. But what came next sealed his fate.

Fitzpatrick asked permission to pack clothing and say goodbye to his mother. It was given.

"When they reached the dwelling," related the *Chester Evening News* in an 1881 article, "Fitzpatrick opened the door and grasped his rifle from behind it, leveled it at the soldiers and swore he would kill them if they did not leave immediately." Then Fitzpatrick returned to his haying.

In late August, Fitzpatrick turned up at the camp of Howe's army, which had landed in Maryland. Fitzpatrick became its guide and may have been the man who volunteered that the Brandywine could be forded north of its Chadds Ford crossing. The British used that information at Brandywine. In that battle, Washington's army barely escaped when the enemy in his front turned out to be also in his rear.

With Howe in Philadelphia, Fitzpatrick staged raids into Chester County, confiscating property from known Patriots and identifying himself as "Captain Fitz." (Whether the title was official is disputed.) When the British departed in 1778, however, he faced a choice: formally join the British army—whose discipline was nastier than that of the Americans—or continue his own freelance war. He and a partner chose the latter.

"They made their headquarters near a point known as Hand's Pass, near the present town of Coatesville," reported the *Chester News*, "and… rendered their names a terror to the Whigs of that neighborhood." The two men targeted tax officials, whose jobs included collecting the punitive extra taxes applied to those who refused military service or to swear loyalty to the new government.

"Unfortunate tax gatherers who fell in their way were made the victims of the utmost brutality," recorded the newspaper. "Frequently, after stripping them of all their money, they would tie the unhappy officials to convenient trees and flog them unmercifully."

On one occasion, Fitzpatrick was walking down a lonely road when he fell in with two collectors armed with muskets. Had he seen Fitzpatrick? (No, replied Fitzpatrick.) As they walked along and the officials boasted how they would capture the thief, they suddenly found the stranger pointing his gun at their heads. Fitzpatrick took their money and, from one, a Captain McGowan, a sword, pistols and a watch. (He returned the watch when told it was a family heirloom.) Fitzpatrick then tied and whipped both men, but not before clipping off McGowan's prided queue, the braided ponytail worn by eighteenth-century men. The incident became a local ballad:

> *Some he did rob, then let them go free;*
> *Bold Captain McGowan he tied to a tree.*
> *Some he did whip and some he did spare;*
> *He caught Captain McGowan and cut off his hair.*

Fitzpatrick's brazenness and luck infuriated and, perhaps, intimidated the Patriots. He was shot at several times but escaped. In Kennett Square, he walked into a tavern where more than twenty men were planning his capture. Fitzpatrick ordered and downed a drink before he was recognized and then drew his pistol, backed out the door and reached the woods. Still another time, he disguised himself to attend another meeting called to form a posse.

"A young militia captain had a great deal to say about how he would seize him," wrote Penn State historian Rosemary S. Warden. "The unarmed Fitzpatrick…told the unsuspecting young man that if he would come outside with him, he would show him how to catch the robber." Outside, Fitzpatrick fooled the man into thinking a candlestick was a pistol and then took his watch, tied his hands and pushed him back into the meeting to share what had happened.

Fitzpatrick's gallantry was admired. He returned some eggs to a woman who protested that she was poor and needed them to sell. Another time, he identified himself to a Newtown Square blacksmith but still paid the full bill for reshoeing his horse.

Patriot officials, in contrast, seemed both incompetent and mean: a militiaman turned over Fitzpatrick's mother's house searching for him, and broke her spinning wheel in the process.

He was captured, of course—pounced on by an Edgmont homeowner and his servant girl when Fitzpatrick laid down his pistol in the midst of trying on the owner's shoes. The homeowner, militia captain Robert McFee, shared the state's $1,000 reward with Rachel Walker but later paid with the loss of his barn, burned by a Fitzpatrick sympathizer. (The McFee home, on West Chester Pike, was bulldozed in the 1990s for the Edgmont Square Shopping Center.)

Fitzpatrick was convicted in a one-day trial at which, wrote Taylor, "he looked around the court-room with his usual defiant air."

Patriot officials preferred to treat men like Fitzpatrick as criminals rather than as prisoners of war. Congress had decreed in 1777 that all native-born individuals serving the British should be turned over to their states for punishment. In Pennsylvania, Chief Justice Thomas McKean ruled that anyone who chose the British side before February 1777 was a prisoner of war, not a criminal. McKean's ruling wouldn't have saved Fitzpatrick, who had deserted in 1776. But what is revealing is Patriot officials' efforts to evade the ruling to punish their enemies.

In 1780, the Americans captured Lieutenant Samuel Chapman of Bucks County, who had been in the British service since 1776. Patriot officials tried to bring a charge of treason against Chapman, whose real crime seems to have been that he defeated American general John Lacey in a 1778 skirmish. Lacey was a member of Pennsylvania's ruling executive council. McKean invoked his earlier ruling, and Chapman was eventually exchanged.

Fitzpatrick, however, was hanged from a tree at Edgmont and Providence Avenues with a rope several feet too long. "When the cart was pulled out from under him, his feet dangled so low that he was able to…[stand] on his toes," wrote Warden. At this, the executioner leaped forward and—depending on the account one reads—either pushed down or stood on Fitzpatrick's shoulders. Those in attendance, including many officials and Fitzpatrick's mother, were allowed to see him slowly strangle. (In 1906, in a similarly botched execution in Minnesota, this took fifteen minutes.)

Couldn't they have measured the rope? Or did they?

1813: Empathy

Familiarity does not breed contempt; it breeds empathy. People who know Muslims don't fear Muslims. Support for same-sex marriage is greater among those who know someone gay.

Familiarity also explains the abolitionist career of Thomas Garrett (1789–1871), who returned to his parents' Upper Darby home one day in 1813 and found the place in an uproar. An African American employee—referred to in some accounts as "Mary"—had been seized, thrown into a wagon and taken away by men who insisted that she was a runaway slave.

Accounts of Mary's household duties are vague. However, Garrett's parents had thirteen children, so they certainly needed a lot of help. Mary was likely someone who washed Thomas Garrett's clothes, cleaned the house and cooked and served his meals. That connection likely explains his outrage. Garrett followed the wagon by its distinctive track, found the woman and her captors in Kensington and brought Mary home. Then, he devoted the rest of his life to liberating as many slaves as possible. A few years later, he moved to Wilmington, where he became one of the most prominent figures in the Underground Railroad. Late in his life, Garrett personally claimed to have helped more than 2,700 slaves escape over a forty-year career.

"What he promised, he fulfilled," wrote abolitionist William Lloyd Garrison on the occasion of Garrett's death. "What he attempted, he seldom or never failed to accomplish; what he believed, he dared to proclaim upon the housetop; what he ardently desired and incessantly longed for, was the reign of universal peace and righteousness."

When slave catchers raided Riverview, the Garretts' Upper Darby farm, in 1813, they grabbed Mary, a family employee Thomas Garrett knew and cared about. Garrett rescued Mary and then devoted his life to freeing as many runaway slaves as possible. *Courtesy of Robert Seeley.*

The Garretts were a prolific Quaker family whose founder, a miller named William Garat, had arrived in Pennsylvania from Leicestershire in 1684. By the time Thomas Garrett was born just over a century later, four generations had passed with eight to ten children each. As a result, Garretts were spread across most of Delaware and Chester Counties.

Thomas Garrett Sr., a farmer and manufacturer of edge tools (scythes, axes, knives, chisels, etc.), had inherited 284-acre Riverview Farm, a remnant of the original estate that included William Garat's seventeenth-century farmhouse. And it was there that Thomas, the sixth of eleven children born to his father's second wife, Sarah Price Garrett, was raised. (Demolished in 1969, the site of the farmhouse on Shadeland Avenue is now a playground for the School of the Holy Child Jesus.)

During Garrett's boyhood, slavery was not yet the sectional flashpoint issue that it would later become. Indeed, the institution seemed to be dying,

Convicted and stiffly fined in 1848 for helping runaway slaves escape, Thomas Garrett defiantly announced, "If anyone knows a fugitive who wants a shelter and a friend, send him to Thomas Garrett." *Courtesy of Boston Public Library.*

as many of the Founding Fathers had hoped it would. Stiff competition against American rice, indigo and tobacco growers made slavery steadily less profitable. Quakers such as the Garretts, of course, had been forbidden by their church to own slaves since 1776.

But in 1793, when Garrett was a toddler, Eli Whitney invented the cotton gin. The device greatly accelerated the processing of raw cotton, allowing producers to cut prices and expand markets. In 1792, the year before Whitney's invention, the United States exported a mere 138,328 pounds of cotton. "This put her on the same level as a producer as Guiana," wrote historian Hugh Thomas. In 1820, cotton exports reached 35 million pounds. Gradually, cotton became the South's major cash crop.

Greater production required more slaves. In 1790, there were only 500,000 slaves in the United States. Between 1800 and 1810, this number increased by one-third; between 1810 and 1820, by another third. Cotton became the most important U.S. export, causing an unprecedented demand for slaves. As that demand accelerated, slave populations in the Upper South actually declined somewhat as workers were traded to the Deep South, where cotton was grown. Female slaves were particularly desired, wrote Thomas, because "it was supposed that the sensitive harvesting of cotton demanded female labor."

Much is often made of the fact that the Garretts were Quakers. But most Quakers did not participate in the Underground Railroad, an illegal activity that Friends, as a group, would officially condemn as leading toward violence. At the time, the proper outlet for antislavery Quakers was the Pennsylvania Abolition Society (PAS), founded in 1784.

PAS activities were confined mostly to annual petitions to Congress to ban the slave trade and providing lawyers for kidnapped African Americans who were legally free. For those legally enslaved, PAS had little to offer. PAS's most prominent members included Founding Fathers Benjamin Franklin and Benjamin Rush, which may partially explain its conservatism.

Slave owner George Washington bemoaned PAS activities. In a 1786 letter, he described the escape of a Virginia neighbor's slave to Philadelphia, where "a society of Quakers in the city, formed for such purposes, have attempted to liberate" him. Reviled by proslavery forces as radical and by abolitionists as timid, PAS faded away after the 1833 founding of the more radical American Anti-Slavery Society.

Garrett joined PAS in 1818 but eventually moved beyond its careful philosophy. He moved to Wilmington in 1822, a relocation that some biographers think was more about antislavery strategy than about business. There, he went into business as an iron, steel, coal and hardware retailer.

"Why Wilmington?" asked Garrett biographer James A. McGowan. "Why not Chester, or York or any other city in the free state of Pennsylvania?" McGowan credited the Upper Darby kidnapping attempt and its profound effect on Garrett's life priorities. "With such a life's purpose revealed to him," he concluded, "it would simply be a matter of course for a man of Thomas Garrett's bold character to pack up and, in today's vernacular, 'be where the action is.'"

But that grit also served his business. According to a nineteenth-century biographer, William Tilden, a competing iron dealer tried to crush Garrett early in his career by reducing its prices to cost. In response, Garrett undercut *that* price.

Wrote Tilden: "Friend Thomas, nothing daunted, employed a man to take his place in the store, tied on his leather apron, took to his hammer and anvil and, in the prosecution of the trade he had learned from his father, prepared to support his family with his own hands so long as the run lasted."

That brazen determination came into full form in Garrett's single-minded battle with slavery. Delaware was, of course, a slave state. But by the time a runaway reached Wilmington, he or she did not have far to go to reach free territory. "Pursuit by the enraged slave-owner in [border] states was often hot and ruthless," wrote McGowan, noting that those suspected of harboring runaways not infrequently had their homes burned and were themselves tarred and feathered.

And yet, Garrett worked at his illegal and controversial hobby for decades without harm. In 1853, he was slightly bruised when three men tried to throw him off a train that he had boarded to save a free black woman from being carried south. And despite the rough treatment, he retrieved the woman. Garrett attributed his luck to his age, his Quakerly appearance and his "cool impudence."

Garrett never worked alone but rather with allies, both black and white. Allies to the south funneled fugitives to his door; allies to the north received those he sent on; allies across the nation and abroad sent money to help finance it all, though Garrett spent plenty of his own.

In 1857, Garrett wrote to an English supporter, describing how—with the help of her "handsome donation"—he had reunited a family of runaways. The father, he told Mary Edmundson, "a man of noble form," had left his wife and three daughters in Virginia and traveled more than three hundred miles to reach Wilmington in the fall of 1855. There, Garrett sent him on to Massachusetts. The rest of the family fled separately, spent the winter hiding in a cave and reached Garrett in the spring of 1856. When the woman despaired of ever seeing her husband again, Garrett asked the man's name and told his wife where to find him. "I enjoyed their happiness as much as I ever enjoyed a Quaker meeting with the best of preachers," wrote Garrett. "In 36 hours, she was with her husband."

Among Garrett's favorite allies was Harriet Tubman (circa 1820–1913), an escaped slave herself who made repeated trips south to lead others to freedom. Tubman was a frequent visitor at the Garretts' Shipley Street home, and Garrett wrote glowing accounts of her adventures while also worrying about her safety.

Usually, Tubman asked for money. In 1856, wrote Garrett, "Harriet came into my office and addressed me thus: 'Mr. Garrett, I am here again, out of money and with no shoes to my feet and God has sent me to you for what I need.'" She got it.

Garrett's worst disaster came in 1848, when he was convicted of helping a fugitive family from Maryland to escape. The judge was Roger B. Taney, chief justice of the U.S. Supreme Court and, in 1857, author of the Dred Scott decision that blacks had "no rights a white man was bound to respect."

Admonished to stop breaking the law, Garrett reportedly replied, "Judge, thou has not left me a dollar, but I wish to say to thee, and to all in this courtroom, that if anyone knows a fugitive who wants a shelter and a friend, send him to Thomas Garrett."

Why the defiance? It all started in 1813, when slave catchers seeking more female cotton pickers came to Upper Darby.

1847: Listen to the Tadpoles Sing

Scripture tells us to "make a joyful noise unto the Lord" and to "come before His presence with singing" (Psalm 100:1–2).

It seems simple enough, until you worry the details: Exactly when should we sing? And, if we are always in His presence, when not? Who determines when we are joyful? How should we know when to "shout" (another translation of "noise") and when to whisper?

In 1847, such questions sparked a schism at Bethel Methodist Church, which served southern Delaware and neighboring New Castle Counties. Progressives and younger people brought in a new hymnal featuring, for the first time, the musical scale, which told members what their voices should do. Old-timers, thinking this smacked almost of popery, left to form a new church up the road. "I know people whose grandparents wouldn't talk to each other because their grandparents had been on opposite sides of this," said James Hanby, the unofficial historian of the splinter church, Siloam Methodist.

Sarah Foulk Clayton might have predicted trouble from the rowdy Methodists. Recounting the church squabble in an 1892 memoir, Thomas Jefferson Clayton (1826–1900), a Delaware County judge and member of Bethel Methodist, recalled that his grandmother had "despised" the Methodists for the noisy, shouting emotionalism of their worship.

"When my grandfather became a Methodist," wrote Clayton, "she thought the family disgraced. She shut herself up in her room over a week and wept from shame." After eight days, Sarah relented and again "received her husband with her wonted grace." But before she died—

Old-time Methodists thought worship should be spontaneous. So, the specter of church choirs like this one—with members singing from books and even playing instruments—was horrifying. One local church split over the issue. *Courtesy of Library of Congress.*

possibly in childbirth—in 1795, she made her husband promise to bury her in a Quaker burial ground, though she was not a Friend, rather than let her lie among Methodists.

Organized Methodism arrived in the Mid-Atlantic region with church pioneer Thomas Webb (1724–1796), a former British army officer who first came to America in 1758 to take part in the siege of Louisburg and later published *A Military Treatise on the Appointments of the Army*. (Comparing warfare in the New and Old Worlds, Webb argued that America's rough terrain demanded lighter weapons to maintain mobility. George Washington's copy of Webb's treatise is in a Boston museum.) Webb was known for laying both his sword and his Bible on the pulpit as he preached.

Personally converted by John Wesley, the founder of Methodism, Webb retired from the military in 1766 to become one of the church's first American evangelists. In 1767, he founded the first Methodist society in Philadelphia and two years later, preached at New Castle and Wilmington. In 1780, inspired by Webb's visits, border-area Methodists built a log meetinghouse— Cloud's Chapel, after Robert Cloud, who donated the land—on Foulk Road, just south of the Pennsylvania-Delaware line in New Castle County. When the log structure was replaced by a stone church in 1799, the congregation became known as Bethel Methodist Episcopal Church.

Methodists like to sing. Wesley himself wrote hymns. His more prolific brother, Charles, wrote more than seven thousand. But the denomination also bore the marks of the English Reformation which, in the sixteenth and seventeenth centuries, had disbanded monasteries, smashed stained-glass windows and statues, painted over ancient frescoes and translated the Bible to English for the laity—all to make religion more accessible to the average person.

Musically, Martin Luther (1483–1546) set the pace when he eliminated Catholic polyphony—music sung by multiple trained singers, including those famous castrati—and restored congregational singing. In earlier times, the Catholic Church allowed congregations to sing doxologies, hymns and amens but, in the late sixth century, transferred the song of the church to professionals under the direction of the clergy. Luther's objection wasn't that the professionals didn't sing well but that they deprived the congregation of an opportunity to sing at all—and thus of an opportunity to participate in the liturgy.

When modernists introduced hymnals including the musical scale at Chester-Bethel Methodist Church in 1847, one outraged member insisted that "black and white tadpoles, some with their tails up, some with their tails down…trying to crawl through the fence… [was] all the work of the devil." *Courtesy of Chester-Bethel Methodist Church.*

English Puritans were more austere than Luther. They simply sang the psalms. Even more severe were the Baptists and the Quakers, who considered music a distracting frill and eliminated it. Baptists later introduced psalm singing, but a schism over "man-made" songs wasn't healed until a London pastor published a book of approved hymns in 1691.

Like the Baptists, Methodists used approved hymnals, but those books contained only song texts. There were no musical scales, which would have been useful only to professional musicians. Mostly, recalled Clayton, the Methodists shouted their own inspired praises or remembered songs. Many were illiterate and, thus, unable to read the hymnals anyway.

"Methodism, in those days, was much more primitive than it now is," he wrote. "The early Methodists did not condemn shouting aloud their praises to the Lord. They sung and prayed with great spiritual fervor and did not believe in [orchestrated] church music or educated preachers. They regarded religion as a *faith* rather than as a *philosophy*."

It worked. According to Clayton, Bethel Church in 1847 was among "the most flourishing" in Delaware. The stone meetinghouse was crowded most Sundays, and winter revivals overflowed. Night services were needed to manage the crowds.

The congregation possessed several good singers but no regular church choir. What Bethel Methodist did have was a singing society of mostly young people who practiced at one another's homes.

That the singers were young may, in itself, have made their elders suspicious. Were they wholly focused on worship or on each other? Some evidence suggests, at least, a mixture of motives. In 1855, for instance, Horatio C. King, a freshman at Dickinson College in Carlisle, wrote of his hymnal adventures in a diary later published as *Journal of My College Life: Comprising love, foolishness and the like*.

"Ordered two pieces of music," wrote King, "[and] also received the *Lute of Zion*, the [hymnal] wich [*sic*] we intend to learn from. Went down to Mrs. Porter's again tonight. Had a splendid time…Miss Sallie is still very kind and sisterlike to me. I love her dearly. Mattie and Fannie looked beautiful as usual. I love them both…We cut up considerable in [Hymn] No. 33, singing &c…Retired to dream of all the Porter family at 11 o'cl."

The *New Lute of Zion*, blamed in some accounts for what happened at Bethel Methodist, featured cross-denominational (read: non-Methodist) songs and the musical scale. It also featured polyphonic music—with parts for men and women—that may have seemed both reminiscent of Catholic practice and highly erotic. To innocent country boys, the harmony of the girls' sweet falsettos—and their own oppositional bass voices—may have seemed as exciting as a pole dance.

The *Lute*, however, was not published until 1856, so the Bethel youth were using another hymnal in 1847. Whatever its name, the book's musical scale was an issue when the words started to fly. "About this time," wrote Clayton, "the singers petitioned the trustees…to set apart two benches prepared by a four-inch-wide board nailed upon the back of each bench, for their especial use."

The board was to hold the singing society members' hymnals as they sang. The trustees agreed, but many members of the congregation did not. Older, more primitive Methodists looked on this as a step toward ritualism and high-church practice. Where was the equality of all believers if a few were catered to in this way? Where was the authentic worship that sprang from the soul rather than a book printed in Boston or Philadelphia?

"The friends and enemies of the choir…soon became divided into separate parties," wrote Clayton. "Friends of a lifetime became enemies; families were divided; law suits were engendered; church trials were instituted; in a word, the Devil, under the guise of a note book, entered and ruined the church."

Left unstated, according to Hanby, may have been another issue: slavery. "It's nothing I can prove," he said, "but many twenty-somethings of that era were aggressive about social change. He thinks they may have pushed choir singing as a proxy for abolitionism, another radical issue that made their elders cautious.

But anti-hymnal beliefs were strongly felt. Clayton, then twenty-one and pro-hymnal, later wrote of stopping at the blacksmith shop of anti-hymnal Samuel Grubb. Grubb, "very much excited" over the issue, expressed an intention to take his hammer to church to knock the book rests off the benches. Clayton tried to reason with him.

"I cited David and his harp," he wrote, "the music of the spheres, and even quoted Shakespeare's opinion of 'the man that had no music in his soul.'" Grubb was not impressed.

"Anybody with common sense," retorted the blacksmith, "ought to know that it will not help the voice to look, when you sing, upon those things you call keys and bars, with black and white tadpoles, some with their tails up, some with their tails down, decorated with black flags, and trying to crawl through the fence. It's all the work of the devil."

Hymnal anxiety has not disappeared. In 2003, U.S. Methodists were roiled over hymnal supplement *The Faith We Sing*, which conservatives disliked because some its thousand songs refer to the Deity's feminine characteristics.

At Bethel Methodist, the singers won. The book rests, the hymnals and the "tadpoles" stayed, even as many members left. In 1852, Samuel Hance and Samuel Hanby—remembered locally as First and Second Samuel—donated 1.5 acres at Booth's Corner for a new stone church. The defectors named it Siloam after a pool near Jerusalem whose waters were said to cure blindness.

None of this history prevented Siloam—in 1880, only twenty-eight years later—from organizing its first choir and installing its first organ. Today, the two congregations gather together again twice annually for worship and singing from their tadpole-filled hymnals.

People have to sing, you know.

1850: Got Lightning Rods?

Fear is a great marketing tool but requires plausible danger to keep customers motivated. Burglar-alarm companies need burglars. Manufacturers of bicycle locks count on bicycle thieves. Auto manufacturers require a few lemons to sell extended warranties. If bad things don't happen, sales fall.

In the nineteenth century, that's what happened to manufacturers of lightning rods. Disasters like the 1850 lightning strike that killed three people at a Delaware County estate sale were just too infrequent.

On August 8, 1850, near Village Green in Aston Township, Nathan Dutton and Richard Slawter died minutes after being struck. John McClay was injured. Dutton's mother, Rachel, was not struck. But she was so grief-stricken that she collapsed and died within the hour.

Such incidents are rare. According to the National Lightning Safety Institute, the odds that any particular building will be struck by lightning are about once in 200 years. The chance of an individual being struck: one in 280,000.

For business purposes, that's just not enough danger. Few took the hazard of lightning seriously. Many were annoyed by the scare tactics of lightning rod salesmen, who sold door-to-door and often did shoddy installation work. Poorly installed lightning rods can be more dangerous than no rods at all. Most homeowners just bought insurance.

The lightning rod was invented a full century before the 1850 incident by Benjamin Franklin, who may have been less fascinated with lightning had he lived in an area with fewer summer storms. In 1743, Franklin was first to deduce that storms on the American East Coast traveled there from the southwest, despite contrary evidence from their winds, and formed from rising air masses.

Two years before his famous 1752 kite experiment, Franklin watched a sharp needle turn electricity away from a charged sphere. From this, he theorized that lightning might be prevented with an elevated iron rod connected to the earth to empty static from a cloud: "May not the knowledge of this power of points be of use to mankind, in preserving houses, churches, ships, etc., from the stroke of lightning, by directing us to fix, on the highest parts of those edifices, upright rods of iron made sharp as a needle…Would not these pointed rods probably draw the electrical fire silently out of a cloud before it came nigh enough to strike, and thereby secure us from that most sudden and terrible mischief!"

Additional experiments in Europe confirmed Franklin's theory, which he announced in *Poor Richard's Almanac* in 1753. After a Philadelphia house equipped with such a rod survived a direct strike undamaged, lightning rods became common in the American colonies. When the Darby fire company was organized in 1775, members were allowed to borrow any of its ladders in order to erect lightning rods, provided they were returned within three days.

Despite its success, some viewed Franklin's device as a hazard, claiming that the pointed rods he favored actually attracted lightning to a building. These scientists advocated blunt-ended lightning rods, which, they felt, would conduct away lightning yet not attract it.

The debate eventually became political. During the Revolution, King George III, who associated Franklin's pointed rod with the rebellious American colonies, announced his preference for blunt-ended rods. This caused the East India Company to remove the pointed rods from its powder magazines in Sumatra, one of which was later destroyed by lightning. Not until the 1830s, after more than 220 ships of the British navy were damaged or lost as a result of lightning strikes during the Napoleonic Wars, did the admiralty install Franklin's rods on its sailing ships.

More serious objections came from clergy who felt that lightning rods defied divine will. For centuries, Christian churches had taught that thunder and lightning were signs of God's displeasure—and that, if He destroyed a building with a lightning bolt, He did so for a reason.

In America, a 1755 earthquake was widely attributed to Franklin's rod. The Reverend Thomas Prince, pastor of Old South Church in Boston, wrote that the frequency of earthquakes was due to the large number of "iron points" discharging into the ground. "In Boston are more erected than anywhere else in New England," he wrote, "and Boston seems to be more dreadfully shaken. Oh! there is no getting out of the mighty hand of God."

Three years later, John Adams related a conversation with a Boston physician who "began to prate upon the presumption of philosophy in erecting iron rods to draw the lightning from the clouds. He railed and foamed against the points and the presumption that erected them. He talked of presuming upon God, as Peter attempted to walk upon the water, and of attempting to control the artillery of heaven."

To this, Franklin responded in his matter-of-fact way that no religious objection existed to roofs on buildings to resist precipitation. Therefore, there was nothing wrong with protecting buildings and people against lightning.

Complicating the conservatives' arguments was the undeniable fact that church buildings—tall and often built on hilltops—suffered most from lightning. Gradually, church opposition softened. For Catholics, the turning point was the destruction in 1769 of the Church of San Nazario at Brescia in Italy. Fourteen years after Franklin announced his discovery, the Republic of Venice had stored twenty tons of gunpowder in the church's vaults and refused to install a lightning rod. The church was struck by lightning, and the gunpowder exploded. One-sixth of the city was destroyed, and an estimated three thousand people were killed. Thereafter, most churches used lightning rods.

Having survived such challenges, however, the lightning rod was effectively done in by the excesses of American capitalism. Part of the blame belongs to Franklin: rather than patent his device, he offered the idea free to the public. Franklin even published instructions to help do-it-yourselfers build their own lightning rods at home. Later, during the Industrial Revolution, entrepreneurs created a mass market for factory-made rods.

It was the "market revolution," a period in which increasing numbers of Americans became more tied to a cash economy and market values. Franklin's rod became a status symbol. Competing manufacturers added balls, whorls, finials and other decorative devices to attract consumers who saw the lightning rod as an architectural statement of a homeowner's modern, scientific outlook. The ornamental glass balls were intended to shatter, thus indicating which rod had been struck so the owner could check it and the grounding wire for damage.

But the sales tactics turned people off. Lightning rods were sold door to door by characters with no shame. Herman Melville's *The Lightning Rod Man* (1854) described a pitch by a salesman who came to his door in a thunderstorm.

1850: Got Lightning Rods?

"Will you order one of my rods?" the huckster demanded. "Look at the specimen, sir. One rod will answer for a house so small as this. Look over these recommendations. Only one rod, sir; cost, only twenty dollars. Hark! There go all the granite Taconics and Hoosics dashed together like pebbles. By the sound, that must have struck something. An elevation of five feet above the house will protect twenty feet radius all about the rod. Only twenty dollars, sir—a dollar a foot. Hark—Dreadful!—Will you order? Will you buy? Shall I put down your name? Think of being a heap of charred offal, like a haltered horse burnt in his stall; and all in one flash!"

Disgusted, Melville broke the device over his knee and threw it and the salesman out of his house.

In the 1880s, a Texas newspaper described how a lightning rod salesman conned one homeowner. Invited to pitch his product at lunch, the salesman burst into tears at the table. "I used to have a pretty little daughter just like yours," he sobbed, "and then a storm came and lightning hit my house. It killed my little daughter and burned up my house." The homeowner bought two lightning rods.

Perhaps such shenanigans explain why there was no lightning rod on the Village Green house in which Slawter and the Duttons found themselves on that day so long ago. As they browsed the goods, a storm came up. According to the *Delaware County Republican*, lightning entered the peak of the roof and passed down between the clapboards and the plaster.

At the first floor, it divided,

one portion passing in at a hook driven in the wall, from which a looking-glass was suspended, and striking Nathan P. Dutton, who was standing under the glass, upon the top of the head, leaving but a slight mark. The fluid passed to his left arm above the elbow, thence down his body, burning the skin in its passage. He lived about five minutes, and was sensible of his approaching dissolution. The fluid passed from him to John McClay, who was standing near, struck him in the back, and ran down both his legs, burning the skin and clothes from his body, tearing his shoes to fragments and leaving a small hole in the toe of one of them, as if perforated by a bullet.

The other branch of the fluid struck Richard P. Slawter, who was standing outside of the house, and felled him to the ground. He was taken up, but expired in about fifteen minutes. Rachel Dutton, the mother of Nathan, was in an adjoining room, and, on being told of the fate of her son, she came out and immediately commenced to render every assistance in her power to restore him to animation. After laboring with great anxiety for nearly half an hour, she gradually fainted away and, continuing to lose respiration, she expired in about three-quarters of an hour after the death of her son.

Sure, a new store-bought lightning rod could have prevented the tragedy. But that would have meant succumbing to the fearmongers and, thereby, being less than our best selves. And some things are worse than death.

1855: Ellwood Takes a Drive

Among nonprofits, this is the age of collaboration. Organizations applying for grant money are often told to find partners that will share expenses and resources. Donors believe they get more bang for their buck from group efforts. In 2007, for instance, when the Philadelphia Museum of Art opened a major Wyeth exhibit, it partnered with Atlanta's High Museum of Art, borrowed paintings from dozens of institutions and was supported by three big corporate donors.

One stone. Whole buncha birds.

It's not a new strategy. In 1855, Ellwood Harvey, MD (1820–1889), of Delaware County found a way to benefit two good causes with one long carriage ride. Dean of faculty at the struggling Female (later Woman's) Medical College of Pennsylvania (FMCP), Harvey knew his students needed a $300 anatomical dummy to substitute for hard-to-get cadavers. In addition, Harvey, who opposed slavery, learned that abolitionists had offered $300 to whomever rescued a runaway slave hiding from her master near Washington, D.C.

One stone, two birds. Harvey picked up a disguised Ann Maria Weems in the 1600 block of Pennsylvania Avenue, collected the reward and bought his students their device.

Born in Chadds Ford, Harvey was the eldest of his parents' four children. But both Eli and Rachel (Hollingsworth) Harvey had been married previously and brought children from those marriages. The house was always full, and perhaps, the experience alerted Harvey early to the need to prepare for a paying career.

Ellwood Harvey, MD, was a busy man, involved in both women's medical education and the antislavery movement. In 1855, he found a way to help both causes with one long carriage ride. *Courtesy of Steve Harvey.*

In the process, he broke from his family in several respects. His parents were Quakers, but Harvey became an Episcopalian. Eli Harvey was a maltster, but the son set his eye on medicine, graduating from the University of Pennsylvania medical school in 1843. He paid his way by giving lectures to younger students.

Harvey's decision to attend medical school was typical of his generation. For centuries, beginning physicians had mastered their craft like beginning carpenters—as apprentices who worked with established professionals and learned on the job. No academic training was required.

Harvey was part of what social historians William Strauss and Neil Howe remember as the Transcendental Generation—idealistic, even extremist and unusually focused on social progress. Born between 1792 and 1821, Transcendentalists included John Brown, Abraham Lincoln, Robert E. Lee and Susan B. Anthony.

Harvey was all about progress. In addition to getting his own medical education the modern way, he helped to professionalize medicine throughout Delaware County. In 1850, Harvey was one of three physicians who called the organizational meeting of the Delaware County Medical Society. Significantly, the society was open only to medical school graduates—a policy intended, over time, to encourage newcomers to seek formal education.

In 1845, Harvey represented Birmingham Township at a public meeting to consider "the propriety of removing the [county seat] to a more central position." County government had been at Chester since Delaware County was formed in 1789. And for most of those years, residents of the northern townships had complained that Chester was too far away. Harvey initially opposed the move, he wrote, "in accordance with my own convictions and the instructions of my constituents." However, he eventually switched sides and voted to give residents their say in a referendum. "I thought Media would be a miserably poor place and Chester very prosperous," Harvey later wrote. "Media has done better than I expected, and so has Chester."

In 1853, Harvey became nationally known for an 1845 letter he had written to the abolitionist *Pennsylvania Freeman* newspaper, describing his revulsion at a slave auction he had witnessed in Virginia. "The slaves were told they would not be sold," wrote Harvey, "and were collected in front of the quarters, gazing on the assembled multitude. The land being sold, the auctioneer's loud voice was heard, 'bring up the niggers.'" The women, he wrote, snatched up their babies and ran screaming into the huts. The children hid. The men stood in despair. The auctioneer announced that no warranties were included.

$500 REWARD.

R AN away on Sunday night, the 23d instant, before 12 o'clock, from the subscriber, residing in Rockville, Montgomery county, Md., my NEGRO GIRL "Ann Maria Weems," about 15 years of age; a bright mullatto; some small freckles on her face; slender person, thick suit of hair, inclined to be sandy. Her parents are free. and reside in Washington, D. C. It is evident she was taken away by some one in a carriage, probably by a white man, by whom she may be carried beyond the limits of the State of Maryland.

I will give the above reward for her apprehension and detention so that I get her again.

sep 29—3t   CHAS. M. PRICE.

Photographed for abolitionist PR purposes in the boys' clothing in which Ellwood Harvey helped her escape, Ann Maria Weems later reached Canada and disappeared. *Courtesy of Steve Harvey.*

"A few old men were sold at prices from $13 to $25," Harvey wrote, "and it was painful to see old men, with beards white with years of toil and suffering...tell of their diseases and worthlessness, fearing they would be bought by traders for the southern market."

The mother of a twelve-year-old boy rushed forward, crying, "My son, oh my boy, they will take away my dear." But she was pushed back in the house, the door shut in her face and the sale went on. "He was sold for about $250," according to Harvey. "The monsters who tore this child from his mother would sell your child and mine if they had the power."

Harvey's letter had already been well circulated in abolitionist circles. In 1853, however, it became truly notorious when Harriet Beecher Stowe included it in *A Key to Uncle Tom's Cabin*, in which she defended her earlier book by citing examples of slavery's brutality. The *Key* listed examples of slaves murdered and brutalized without consequences, along with the statutes that allowed it and statements by church leaders that condoned it.

"Defending her novel led [Stowe] to mount a more aggressive attack on slavery in the South than the novel itself had," wrote University of Virginia historian Stephen Railton, PhD. "In the novel, she works hard to be sympathetic to white southerners as well as black slaves; here, her prose seems much angrier, both morally and rhetorically more contemptuous."

The furor probably explains why Harvey is often referred to simply as "Dr. H" in accounts of his activities. That is how black abolitionist William Still identified the man who brought Weems to his door. That was also how Still identified his family's physician, now known to have been Harvey. Harvey was involved in many respectable activities, but abolitionists were thought to be troublemakers. Perhaps he decided that he didn't need more notoriety.

Educating women as physicians, for instance, involved plenty of notoriety for one man. Founded by Quakers in 1850, FMCP was the world's first medical college for women. Its founders believed that understanding their own bodies was literally a life-or-death necessity for women. Ann Preston, one of the school's first graduates and later its dean, noticed that—in her family of six boys and three girls—all of her brothers had lived, but her two sisters had died. Sedentary and indoor occupations and tightly bound clothes, she decided, were at least partly to blame.

Regardless, the college was not welcomed. In 1858, the Philadelphia Medical Society spoke out against FMCP, thus barring women from educational clinics and medical societies. In 1869, Preston negotiated with Pennsylvania Hospital to allow her students to attend general clinics. The male students greeted them with hisses and paper wads.

Harvey was involved from the beginning. In 1852, he was named professor of "materia medica" (pharmacology) and general therapeutics. In 1853, he added surgery to his schedule after the appointed professor resigned. Next, obstetrics. Then, chemistry. As each (underpaid) professor left, he took over. At times, he seems to have been the only professor. Finally, Harvey became dean of faculty.

Weems, who belonged to a Maryland family, lost her parents and siblings when they were sold in 1853. The rest of the family eventually reached freedom and attempted, through intermediaries, to buy Ann out of slavery. Her owner refused. In the autumn of 1855, friends had her snatched. News of the affair got into the papers and made flight north too risky. By November, she was still hiding in the attic of an elderly Washington lawyer, Jacob Bigelow.

Meanwhile, FMCP students were trying to learn the body's internal arrangement by looking at pictures. A so-called dissection mannequin—a man-made dummy with removable organs—would be an acceptable substitute.

"That the girl ought to be freed was clear to Dr. Harvey's mind," reported a FMCP newsletter, *The Progress*, in 1879. "And it was equally clear that if he was the man to do it, it would be a good deed and he would get the money for his apparatus."

Passing word through his abolitionist network that he was on his way, Harvey took a train to Baltimore, hired a buggy and drove to Washington. Bigelow and his servant "boy," Joe Wright, met him on a curb in front of the White House, within which President Franklin Pierce—though a New Englander—was following a pro-slavery course. (The Pierce administration favored repeal of the Missouri Compromise, which restricted slavery in the Louisiana Purchase, and annexation of Cuba, which would have provided additional slave territory.)

"Joe" climbed in, Harvey snapped the reins and off they went. The pair was challenged at several tollgates and stayed one night at the tavern of a slave owner who joked about Harvey's runaway. Crossing the Susquehanna, Harvey almost lost Weems to a gang of men who doubted her story, until the doctor took off his coat and "called them to account" for troubling his boy. A couple of days later, Harvey delivered Weems to Still's house in Philadelphia. She later reached Buxton, Ontario, and then vanished from history. All that's left is a daguerreotype commissioned by abolitionist Lewis Tappan, showing her in the boy's clothes in which she had escaped. And soon after, FMCP students had their dummy.

Harvey taught two more years at the school and then resigned to focus on his medical practice. "I gave five years to the good cause [and] was compelled by poverty to quit and do something more lucrative," wrote Harvey in 1871 regarding his support for female medical education. "I regret nothing; I claim nothing; I had my reward in moral and intellectual development. My family never suffered, though we were much straightened. I hoped to do my duty and feel satisfied."

One stone. Many birds.

1864: Progress Be Damned

We live in a standardized world. Plug a GE phone into your wall and it will work as well as a phone from Samsung. Mass market CDs sound as good in your car stereo as obscure foreign releases. Your car will run on gas from Sunoco or Wawa.

This kind of standardization makes mass production and communication possible, and we take it for granted. But it is also the product of another era, when broad-minded businessmen like toolmaker William Sellers (1824–1905) of Upper Darby had the clout to convince their peers that standardization was good for all.

Today, businessmen seem to avoid collaboration. In 2005, for instance, all of the high-tech equipment—linear accelerators, computerized axial tomography (CAT) scanners and positron emission tomography (PET) scanners, etc.—with which cancer patients were treated at Main Line Health hospitals came from Varian Medical Systems of Palo Alto, California.

Why a single vendor, when several competing brands were available? According to Rodel Hidalgo, head therapist, the healthcare provider was locked in because Varian's software didn't talk to that of any other manufacturer, and vice versa.

Sellers considered that sort of situation a problem. His idea—proposed in an 1864 speech at the Franklin Institute—was a standard system for threading screws. Until then, every manufacturer made its own, in its own way, and the result of a broken or missing screw was often misery and delay. Sellers's proposal succeeded, which is why the Sellers—or Franklin Institute—Thread today has another name: the U.S. Standard Thread. But

Sellers's real achievement was in selling the notion that there should be a standard at all. In that argument, his success was complete: Today, there are nearly 800,000 global standards, according to the National Institute of Standards and Technology.

It may also be significant that Sellers and many of his machinist peers were either Quakers or from Quaker families. Sent out as apprentices when they were just boys, they became further convinced on the shop floor of the value of what Friends called "useful knowledge." They disdained the theoretical knowledge of college-trained "paper engineers." But they weren't simply blue-collar snobs. Pre–Civil War machinists were among the first users of precise experimentation and science in the shop. The Franklin Institute itself was founded in 1824 because the shop culture elite wanted a place to talk about the latest discoveries and innovations.

Wired magazine writer James Surowiecki compared Sellers and his peers to Silicon Valley's first engineers and programmers, who traded ideas freely because they were more interested in solving problems than in competitive advantage. "In the same way," wrote Surowiecki, "the scientific machinists Sellers was appealing to were devoted to something bigger than their individual companies, something you might as well call 'technological progress.'"

Born at Millbourne, William Sellers was the eldest surviving son of John and Elizabeth (Poole) Sellers. John, a miller, had grown up at Sellers Hall, now the Sellers Memorial Free Library on State Road. Educated in a private school run by his father, William was apprenticed at age fourteen to his uncle, John Morton Poole of Wilmington, Delaware, to become a machinist.

The Sellers were a family of mechanics. William's brother, Nathan, went into business with their father, and after the elder Sellers's death, John Sellers & Son was incorporated as Millbourne Mills. A cousin, James Sellers, partnered with Abraham Pennock as Sellers & Pennock, an early manufacturer of fire engines. Sellers & Pennock revolutionized fire hose when it developed a method to rivet leather strips together to make a hose that was almost leak-proof. Another cousin, George Escol Sellers (1808–1899), built America, the first locomotive of the Philadelphia & Columbia Railroad, in 1835 for use on the Main Line of Public Works. Still another cousin, Coleman Sellers (1827–1907), was a consulting engineer to Cataract Construction Co., which built the hydroelectric plant at Niagara Falls.

Sellers remained with Poole until 1845 and then left to manage Fairbanks, Bancroft & Co., a Quaker-owned machine shop in Providence, Rhode Island. Three years later, he was back in Philadelphia, setting up his own machine shop in Kensington that, as William Sellers & Co., he led as president until his death.

From the beginning, Sellers went his own way. He was among the first to omit decorative features such as pilasters and human busts from his machines. On Sellers machines, form followed function. He also made his products heavier.

Beginning in 1857, Sellers brought out a series of inventions, winning some ninety U.S. patents and many others abroad. The inventions included machine tools, steam injectors, rifling machines, riveters, hydraulic machinery, steam hammers and turntables.

An 1850s Sellers advertisement claimed that its "anti-friction box" allowed one man to turn its largest turntable and pivot bridges, even when loaded with a locomotive and tender.

Another Sellers company, Edge Moor Iron Co., organized in 1868, furnished the ironwork for the main buildings of the 1876 Centennial—including Memorial Hall, now the Please Touch Museum—and the Brooklyn Bridge. In 1873, Sellers reorganized the William Butcher Steel Works, renaming it the Midvale Steel Co., which became a leader in the production of heavy artillery.

By this time, Sellers had apparently left—or been disowned by—the Quakers. During the Civil War, he was a founder of the Union League and helped to organize colored troops.

Sellers's attitude about cross-company collaboration may have been affected by a threatened lawsuit against his cousin when he was just a boy. In 1835, when George Sellers was about finished with his first locomotive, a lawyer, Charles Chauncey, had appeared in his door to announce that Matthias Baldwin, founder of Baldwin Locomotive, had complained of patent infringement. Specifically, Baldwin claimed that George Sellers was using the same "ground metallic joints for steam and water pipes."

George Sellers told Chauncey, a fellow Quaker and friend, that ground joints were widely used and proof of good work. "It was the practice of my father's shop from my earliest recollection," he later wrote in his memoirs. Chauncey told Sellers to worry no more about it and evidently refused to take Baldwin's case. For his part, George Sellers insisted that the incident "produced no estrangement" between him and Baldwin. "Neither of us ever reverted to it," he wrote. But Baldwin's threat sent a chill through the machinist brotherhood. The locomotive maker generally discouraged his workers from the customary free-and-easy exchange of ideas that the machinists relished.

Nuts and bolts first appeared in the mid-1400s, when they were made by hand and very crude. By the mid-nineteenth century, they had improved a great deal but still varied from one manufacturer to another. In England, Joseph Whitworth had proposed a standard screw, but Sellers didn't think much of it.

The two sides of a Whitworth thread formed an angle of fifty-five degrees, and its tip was rounded. The angle was also difficult to measure accurately and required three kinds of cutters and two kinds of lathe. In an April 1864 presentation at the Franklin Institute, Sellers—the organization's newly elected president—proposed a sixty-degree thread angle, which was one angle of an equilateral triangle and could be easily measured. He also proposed flattening Whitworth's rounded top to ensure that nuts and bolts locked into place. A flat thread was something any machinist could produce quickly, efficiently and cheaply with one cutter and one lathe.

Sellers seems to have done some prep work with his audience before delivering his address, "On a Uniform Standard of Screw Threads." When he finished speaking, a Baldwin official immediately popped up to announce that he hoped Sellers "planned to do more than just talk." Algernon Roberts of Pencoyd Iron quickly proposed a committee to compare the Sellers and Whitworth standards. A month later, the committee voted unanimously in favor of the Sellers standard. Machine-tool shops and government agencies across the country received appeals to adopt it.

By 1883, most U.S. railroads were using Sellers's screw thread, including the Pennsylvania Railroad and its main supplier of engines, Baldwin Locomotive. This forced all their suppliers to also use his new screw thread.

Sellers's final victory came nearly forty years after his death. During World War II, as the Germans battled the British Eighth Army in North Africa, tanks broke down on both sides. Bolts and screws wore out and loosened. American factories sent tons of U.S. Standard screws and bolts, but they didn't fit the British tanks. For the rest of the war, U.S. factories ran two separate lines—one for British and one for American screw threads. In 1948, finally, the British abandoned the Whitworth thread.

More than a half century later, at Main Line Health, Hidalgo was enthused about the things that high tech could do. Digital scanners, for instance, produced in ten seconds the images that once took several minutes to acquire in hard copy. And, more important, he could e-mail them to a physician for a quick go-ahead on a procedure that might once have required a return visit.

On the other hand, if a cancer patient transferred to Main Line midway through radiation therapy on non-Varian equipment, the physics department might spend several hours making conversions before continuing the individual's treatment.

"What differentiates them most is the software," said Hidalgo, whose facility treated 380 people in 2005. "And we want absolutely no confusion when we're treating patients."

Any hope for a common standard? Fat chance, says Mark Brager, a spokesman for the Advanced Medical Technology Association. "I see no incentive for them to do that," said Brager, noting that medical equipment changes quickly and no manufacturer wants to spend time or money updating its competitors.

Where is William Sellers when you need him?

1867: Getting Ready
for Martin

Ideas rarely spring from nowhere. Martin Luther King's ideas came from many sources: his experience in the Jim Crow South, his reading of Gandhi and—not least—his training at the Crozer Theological Seminary in Chester.

Loosely affiliated with the Baptists, Crozer, from its beginnings, emphasized the Social Gospel. And the school trained many of the progressive clergy who made it happen—including, most famously, King, who graduated in 1951. Crozer merged with Colgate Rochester Divinity School and moved to upstate New York in 1970.

Before progressives dumped it for secularism, the Social Gospel was a powerful political tool that united liberal activists and clergy behind causes such as temperance, mandatory Sabbath observance (popular with labor to get a day off) and woman's suffrage. Though some of its goals are now in disfavor, the general idea was that social reform was a godly business.

Conservatives, of course, hated churchy social engineering every bit as much as the secular version. Both offended their conviction that, in a world beyond redemption, the best strategy was to sit tight, wait for death and trust that things will improve afterward. Naturally, conservatives also hated the Crozer Theological Seminary.

Crozer's crimes included the absence of a written creed, professors who questioned traditional doctrine, pacifist speakers and the inclusion of non-Christian ideas in the curriculum. King's experience at Crozer incorporated all of these.

But it all started long before. Even at Crozer's founding in 1867, the seminary "was not as warmly received as one might have wished," according

Always theologically edgy, the Crozer Theological Seminary in Chester trained many "Social Gospel" clergy—including, most famously, Martin Luther King, who graduated in 1951. *Courtesy of Delawarecountyhistory.com.*

to former professor Jesse Brown. Local ministers resented its independence. Rather than being founded by the church, the school was funded by the children of industrialist John P. Crozer as a memorial to their father. And Crozer had been somewhat independent himself.

Born at Upland in 1793, Crozer had lost the family farm when his father died in 1816 and he couldn't afford to buy out his siblings. Instead, he took his share, bought an old paper mill, converted it to cotton manufacture and proceeded to get rich. When a flood did $46,000 worth of damage to his factory in 1843, it didn't even affect Crozer's credit.

But Crozer was not a ruthless capitalist. When twelve- and fourteen-hour days were common, Crozer employees worked ten hours, and their children attended classes in a schoolhouse that Crozer built for them. At his own expense, Crozer built a Baptist church at Upland and donated land and money for another at Chester. In 1856, he gave $50,000 to help found Bucknell University and, in 1866, another $20,000 to establish a professorship in English literature. He also contributed money to educate freed slaves and, in particular, African American ministers.

But Crozer went further. An abolitionist, he was an early member—and later president—of the Pennsylvania Colonization Society, which supported the creation of an African state for freed slaves. In 1820, Crozer's brother, Sam, had sailed with eighty former slaves on one of the first ships to what became Liberia. Crozer was also president of the Pennsylvania Training School for Feeble Minded Children at Elwyn; president of the Home for Friendless Children at Philadelphia; and president of the Woman's Hospital, Philadelphia.

Formally a Baptist, Crozer's ecumenical instincts nevertheless made him a critic of that church's practice of closed communion, which excluded anyone not baptized by immersion.

In 1857, Crozer established a teachers' school on a hill overlooking the Delaware at Chester; it survived four years. During the Civil War, Crozer lent the empty building to the Union army, which used it as a hospital for more than 1,700 Union and Confederate soldiers. Shortly after Crozer's death in 1866, his sons donated the structure for use as a seminary. The Crozers gave the school an initial endowment of $250,000 and hired its first president, Henry G. Weston, pastor of a Baptist church in Manhattan.

Weston moved quickly to establish Crozer's independence. As early as 1875, he brought in ministers from other denominations to lecture about their own theologies. He also presided, in 1876, over the enrollment of Crozer's first black student, Henry Mitchell, a graduate of Lincoln University. (The school had never prohibited African Americans, but none applied before Mitchell.)

Most important, though, were the men he brought to the faculty. Lemuel Moss, who during the Civil War had been secretary of the U.S. Christian Commission, a relief organization, came as professor of New Testament interpretation. Robert Macoskey taught church history. Milton Evans, later president, taught Biblical theology. Henry Vedder, a former journalist, introduced the novelty of independent study.

Traditionally educated, the faculty nevertheless valued academic freedom and shared Weston's vision—stated late in his life—of a Christian ministry whose "starting point will be neither the sovereignty of God nor the person of Christ, but the needs of humanity." Weston died in 1909 and was succeeded by Evans, an academic radical who had abandoned textbook recital in favor of seminars in which students discussed their own research. As president, he also started the *Crozer Quarterly*, which became a leading scholarly journal in liberal theological research.

In the early twentieth century, however, it was Vedder who attracted the most attention. Born in 1853 and converted by a camp meeting preacher's images of hellfire, Vedder graduated from the seminary in 1873 and then spent eighteen years writing for Baptist papers. He came to Crozer in the

1890s but continued to write. And when, in his middle age, Vedder began to lean toward modernist concepts, those sentiments inevitably showed up in his work.

In 1908, Vedder published *Our New Testament: How Did We Get It?*, which questioned the Bible's divine inspiration. Wrote Vedder: "The true foundation of the Christian's faith is not a book, but a person...not the New Testament, but Jesus Christ."

Making the case for Biblical primacy was prominent Philadelphia minister George Ferris, and the two men's public arguments eventually divided area Baptists into two camps. Widening the divide were subsequent books, *Socialism and the Ethics of Jesus* (1912), which caused consternation among business leaders, and *The German Reformation* (1914), in which Vedder criticized the Bible's elevation to the status of "paper pope" by Martin Luther and his fellow reformers.

None of this sat well with conservatives, and even today, conservative Christians—especially southern Baptists—point to Vedder as an example of what's wrong with liberals. A Texas pastor quoted Vedder on his church's website for years simply to illustrate "the extent that a man's mind can be taken captive by Satan."

In 1922, Vedder published *Fundamentals of Christianity*, which condemned the concept of vicarious atonement through the death and resurrection of Christ. "It is quite in accord with human indolence that men should look for a salvation to be accomplished in something done for them," wrote Vedder. "The ideal of Jesus is a salvation accomplished by men, not for them, from within, not from without."

For conservatives, this was the last straw: fire Vedder, they told the Crozer board, or they would create a new seminary adhering to orthodox views. Forced to choose, the board supported Vedder. In 1925, conservatives founded Eastern Baptist Seminary, now the parent of Eastern University in St. Davids.

Crozer became still more isolated from local Baptists and lost much financial support. Increasingly, it reinvented itself as an intellectually oriented graduate school of religion and less an institution to train ministers. In 1948, that was exactly what a bookish nineteen-year-old graduate of Morehouse College was seeking.

King had not initially been attracted to the ministry, although he was the son of a minister. As a young teen, he had shocked his Sunday school teacher by questioning the bodily resurrection of Jesus. "I had doubts that religion was intellectually respectable," he told *Time* magazine in its 1964 "Man of the Year" story. "I revolted against the emotionalism of Negro religion, the shouting and the stamping. I didn't understand it and it embarrassed me." Instead, he considered medicine and law.

But he was also outraged by the daily insults that segregation threw at African Americans. "The angriest I have ever been in my life" is how King described the experience of standing for ninety miles on a Macon-to-Atlanta bus after being forced to give his seat to a white passenger in 1943. Only as a minister, he decided, would he be in a position to change such practices.

But few southern schools accepted African Americans, and available black institutions emphasized the religious emotionalism that King abhorred. Morehouse president Benjamin Mays pointed him to Crozer, where he arrived expecting to be a token Negro. Instead, one-third of the students were black.

Crozer fed King's hunger for a Christian philosophy not mired in doctrine. Echoing Vedder's emphasis on the importance of personal change, Professor Kenneth Smith challenged King to "take on the mind of Christ"—that is, to think as Christ thought in order to do as Christ would have done. King initially dismissed as unrealistic the ideas of pacifist lecturer A.J. Muste, but the readings of Gandhi turned him around. "From Gandhi," he later said, "I learned my operational technique."

Four years after leaving Crozer—where Weston had once predicted a ministry focused "on the needs of humanity"—King organized the Montgomery bus boycott.

Whether modern secularism will accomplish as much remains to be seen.

1874: Fear of Splinters

Fear is useful for those with something to sell. Fear of loss sells extended warranties on small appliances. Fear of loneliness sells makeup to insecure girls. Fear sells political candidates. Fear sells wars.

Locally, fear of…um, hemorrhoids once made Chester—former home of Scott Paper—the world capital of toilet paper. Founded in Philadelphia in 1874, Scott invented the rolled form of toilet paper we know today. It also pioneered the use of advertising to position its humble product as a medical necessity.

"Humiliating and extremely painful," read a Scott description of hemorrhoids in a 1930s ad. "These troubles come from harsh, non-absorbent toilet tissue."

Scott dates itself to 1865 when a young attorney, Thomas Seymour Scott (1839–1901), quit a New York law firm and moved to Philadelphia to help start a wholesale paper business that lasted two years. In 1867, Scott brought in his younger brothers, Irvin and Clarence, to help launch a new company.

T. Seymour Scott & Brothers sold straw paper, a coarse product used by food vendors to wrap produce and raw meat. From this, they branched out to sell better wrapping paper, paper bags and other paper products. They did not sell toilet paper.

"Irvin did most of the legwork," wrote Scott historian Robert Spector. "In the morning, Irvin would don his best clothes and go out to take orders from butchers for straw paper. Then, in the afternoon, he would change into his old clothes and deliver orders with his pushcart."

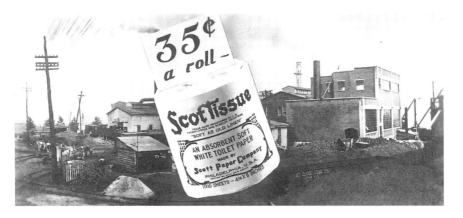

Scott toilet tissue—shown here against the backdrop of its Chester plant in 1910—was the first to be sold in the rolled form familiar today. Scott cornered the market by positioning its product as a medical necessity. © *2007 Kimberly-Clark Worldwide. Used with permission.*

Thomas Scott eventually withdrew from the company. His brothers, meanwhile, saw a new opportunity and founded Scott Paper, specializing in toilet tissue.

Irvin and Clarence Scott were tall, bearded, bespectacled, Victorian gentlemen who worked well together. Clarence, a Sunday school teacher, was a born salesman. Irvin, a Quaker, liked to fish, shoot ducks and smoke cigars. Manufacturing and distribution were his focus. Company literature emphasized the brothers' interest in quality, quoting Irvin that "quality cannot be acquired by good intentions alone, but must actually be built into the products."

But what is quality toilet paper? Scott Paper had an answer.

The need now satisfied by toilet paper is ancient. But little proof exists for most of the widely claimed solutions. Seashells have been cited for people living in coastal communities. For those in the tropics, coconut shells. In medieval Europe, straw and grass. In early America, corncobs.

In 1535, French Renaissance writer Francois Rabelais (circa 1490–1553) published *Gargantua,* a satirical novel in which the title character describes his search for sanitary comfort: "Once I did wipe me," wrote Rabelais, "with a gentlewoman's velvet mask, and found it to be good; for the softness of the silk was very voluptuous and pleasant to my fundament. Another time with one of their hoods, and in like manner that was comfortable; at another time with a lady's neckerchief, and after that some ear-pieces made of crimson satin; but there was such a number of golden spangles in them that they fetched away all the skin off my tail with a vengeance."

Gargantua continues on this subject for several pages before concluding that the best choice was the neck of a live goose, "for you will thereby feel in your nockhole a most wonderful pleasure, both in regard of the softness of the said down, and of the temperate heat of the goose."

Rabelais' book was, of course, fiction. But it does suggest a search to which readers might relate.

Plumbing historian W. Hodding Carter thinks eighteenth-century Americans may have simply wiped themselves with their undergarments. Carter quoted Moreau de St. Mery, a refugee from the French Revolution who arrived in Philadelphia in 1793. St. Mery thought American women excessively modest, writing that they hid their chemises because "they are guilty of not keeping them clean, and of dirtying them with marks of the need to which Nature has subjected every animal." Carter found this persuasive, concluding that the custom of wearing underwear may simply have been inherited from an era in which it served harsher duty.

The first documented use of paper seems to have been in sixth-century China, when an official wrote, "Paper on which there are quotations or commentaries from Five Classics or the names of sages, I dare not use for toilet purposes."

Flushable toilet paper, however, is a byproduct of indoor plumbing. And plumbing, in turn, was a result of a reform craze in the 1840s, when Americans experimented with health-related ideas, including vegetarianism, hydropathy and homeopathy.

"Americans had proved that republicanism could work," wrote Maureen Ogle, another plumbing historian, "and many felt obliged to maintain that example for the edification of the rest of the world." Part of the example was strong families that, in turn, led to increased interest in family homes. In 1856, the editors of *Village and Farm Cottages*—a book of blueprints—put it this way: "He who improves the dwelling-houses of a people in relation to their comforts, habits and morals makes a benignant and lasting reform at the very foundation of society."

Convenience was an important principle in the improved home. Architectural texts touted dish closets, dumbwaiters and a nearby wood house. Municipal water was mostly undeveloped, so wells, pumps and cisterns were deemed essential. Ogle described pre–Civil War arrangements in which an attic water tank used gravity to supply downstairs faucets, a shower and a water closet (WC).

Early WCs featured a metal commode. A few used water to flush wastes down a pipe to a cesspool, said Ogle, but most dropped things into a pit.

In either case, said Ogle, their owners were likely first to conclude that a specialized wiping product might protect their systems.

"People who were quick to plumb their houses tended to be forward-thinking innovators, who embraced progress in all its forms," she said. "Think of them as the same kind of people who today are quick to adopt computers, webcams [and] flat-screen TVs."

For such folks, Joseph Gayetty of New York produced what is thought to have been the first commercial toilet paper in 1857. It carried his watermark and was moistened with aloe. Why aloe? "Nineteenth-Century Americans had a lot of bowel issues," said Ogle. "There were tons of products for constipation, rashes [and] hemorrhoids." The cause, she said, was a greasy diet with lots of tainted meat but irregular supplies of fruits and vegetables.

By the mid-nineteenth century, then, many Americans were living in homes with running water and indoor toilets and were accustomed to pampering their bottoms with specialized products. In the 1870s, when a new group of reformers democratized earlier advancements by building municipal water and sewer systems, the Scotts were in a very good position.

According to company legend, many retailers declined to stock this risqué product unless packaged under their own names. So, for about twenty years, Scott quietly customized its product to meet wholesale specifications. By 1896, it had more than two thousand private-label customers, including John Wanamaker. With the turn of the early twentieth century, however, a new generation—Irvin's son, Arthur—took over.

"Arthur's strategy was to phase out the private-label business," wrote Spector, "and concentrate on a few popular, distinctive Scott-owned brands that could be produced efficiently and consistently." Over the next few years, Scott formed its "Sanitary Line," which emphasized purity. One brand, Sani-Tissue, was treated with balsam. In 1908, to ensure consistency, the company began manufacturing its own paper in Chester. By 1911, branded products totaled 80 percent of Scott's annual sales of $500,000.

Scott was a top brand. It was known to have introduced rolled paper. But a competitor offered the first perforated paper. And Scott probably wasn't the first with soluble paper, which protects pipes by collapsing into nothingness when wet.

The company needed an angle and found one in the precedent of medicated wipes. Before World War I, Scott formed a platoon of inspectors who surveyed consumers, enforced (vague) quality standards and reported directly to Arthur Scott. Packaging depicted female inspectors in crisp white nurse-like uniforms.

Using advertising, Scott defined quantity as part of quality. Until 1915, toilet paper was sold by weight. Scott introduced the idea that a roll should have a guaranteed number of sheets and announced that it would fire workers who produced short rolls.

Most effective, though, were mental images of sore bottoms. Scott touted softness, absorbency and cleanliness, while suggesting what might happen with the wrong brand. "After 40 years of age," warned a 1929 ad, "doctors say you have one chance in two of contracting some form of rectal disease." The cause: "Harsh or impure toilet paper."

But for outraging competitors, nothing topped Scott's aggressive 1930s ads. In one, a mother announced, "I'm taking no chances, with my baby or myself." Another showed a child reporting on a play date: "They have a pretty house, Mother, but their bathroom paper hurts." No competitor was named, but several complained to the FTC anyway.

Northern Tissue fought back by declaring itself "splinter free," but Scott was on top of that game. Between 1926 and 1935, annual production leaped from 67 million rolls to 180 million. By 1939, Chester-based Scott was the world's largest manufacturer and exporter of toilet tissue.

Did anyone ever get a splinter or rash from bad toilet paper? History has not recorded his name. But fear of being that person helped make Scott a success.

1898: Wading in Cold Water

Before the camera, journalism depended upon combat illustrators to show the gritty glory of war. Overall, it could be argued that the illustrators did the better job. Why? Part of the answer can be found in the lessons taught at an old gristmill—now the Chadds Ford Township office building—where Wilmington illustrator Howard Pyle (1853–1911) brought his best students for summer classes at the turn of the twentieth century.

Pyle was a popular artist during "America's Golden Age of Illustration." That era began about 1880 with the development of high-quality printing technology and ended about 1920 with the arrival of radio and the fast-shutter camera. For those few decades, storytellers depended on illustrators for images to help convey their words to a literate and increasingly affluent public.

An important characteristic of this era was the primacy of ideas. Stories came first and then were read by artists who prepared illustrations. These illustrators were not undisciplined free spirits but team players—practically assembly-line workers—responsible for a critical phase of production. For this perceived subservience, snobs have long regarded illustration as a lesser art.

Today, pictures tend to come first. One result is the PR phenomenon known as the "photo op," at which the media is provided with images that then form their content.

Born to Quaker parents who hoped he would study for one of the professions, Pyle launched his career in 1876. To his amazement, *Scribner's Monthly* accepted and published his story about a fretful old parson magically transformed into a terrible boy.

Popular illustrator Howard Pyle was also a teacher who "fought, sang, struggled and sobbed through his work" and—in free summer classes that emphasized feeling—taught his students to do the same. *Courtesy of Library of Congress.*

After several more successes, an editor urged Pyle to move to New York. For three years, he lived and worked in Manhattan, selling illustrated stories to publications such as *Harper's Weekly* and *St. Nicholas*, a children's magazine. In the early 1880s, he moved back to Wilmington, married and opened his own studio, where he fulfilled commissions while also writing and illustrating his own books and articles. During Pyle's career, he wrote and illustrated more than twenty books, including *The Merry Adventures of Robin Hood* (1883), whose success made him famous.

Even a French impressionist was impressed. "Do you know an American magazine called *Harper's Monthly*?" Vincent van Gogh queried his brother, Theo, in 1881. "There are things in it which strike me dumb with admiration, including sketches of a Quaker town in the olden days by Howard Pyle."

Once famous, Pyle became an evangelist for his vision of illustration. In 1894, after the Pennsylvania Academy rejected his offer to teach because it was "for the fine arts only"—there's that snobbery—Pyle began a weekly illustration class at the Drexel Institute of Technology. Two years later, Drexel established a School of Illustration and gave it to Pyle to run.

Because only advanced students were admitted, Pyle taught no technical method. Instead, he focused on developing students' ability to "project" themselves into the situation they were illustrating. "Howard Pyle taught, fought, sang, struggled and sobbed through his work," wrote one of his students, W.H.D. Koerner. He wanted his students to do the same.

This was very different from traditional art classes emphasizing color and design. And though Pyle didn't deny standard principles of illustration, his goal was to show that drama and purpose—ideas—were what made an illustration worthy, not technique.

Almost inevitably, this led to Chadds Ford. Enrollment in Drexel's new school grew quickly, but Pyle soon recognized that only a few students had enough talent to find his teaching useful. His options seemed to be to waste his time, which he disliked, or to ignore those less talented, which Pyle knew would cause resentment.

His initial solution, launched in the summer of 1898 and repeated the following year, was free summer classes for his best students. Pyle liked this intimate setting so much that, in 1900, he resigned from Drexel and established his own school at his Franklin Street studio in Wilmington. Students paid only a prorated fee to cover the interest on Pyle's capital outlays, plus model fees. In 1902, this amounted to $4.90 per month per student. After a hiatus in 1900, the free summer classes at Chadds Ford resumed in 1901 and continued through 1903.

It was both summer camp and boot camp. If Pyle enjoyed the intimacy and lack of distraction at his Wilmington school, his goal at Chadds Ford was to remove even *more* distractions. Here, there'd be none of that bothersome family life and going home for the night to sleep. At the same time, students would be immersed in the raw material of nature that this then-rural area provided.

And the students did work, painting from 8 a.m. to 5 or 6 p.m. in the old mill. Many had bicycles, so there were sketching excursions that roamed the countryside for suitable material. Picnics were common, and there were holiday trips to nearby points of interest such as Valley Forge. Pyle frequently led his students on tramps through the countryside, where he described the beauties of nature as a "reflection of the glory of God." Sketching was constant.

During these summers, Pyle's male students slept at what is now Washington's Headquarters. The women stayed in Lafayette's Headquarters.

Frank Schoonover's depiction of a World War I battle, *Belleau Wood*, suggests—through the terror and pain of its subjects—teacher Howard Pyle's emphasis on feeling. *Courtesy of U.S. Marine Corps Art Collection.*

Pyle, his wife and six children lived in a nearby farmhouse where, every Saturday evening, impromptu parties were held. The porch served as a stage for charades, and after dark, students and family alike gathered inside around the Pyle fireplace.

N.C. Wyeth (1882–1945), father of Andrew, and Maxfield Parrish (1870–1966) are probably Pyle's best-remembered students. But others deserve mention.

Edwin Austin Abbey (1852–1911) decorated McKim, Mead & White's Boston Public Library with a fifteen-panel series, *The Quest for the Holy Grail*, and then went on to an even more massive project creating murals for the recently completed Pennsylvania capitol. When Abbey died during the capitol project, fellow Pyle alum Violet Oakley (1874–1960) took over the commission. Her murals depicting the religious roots of law decorate the Supreme Court chamber.

Elizabeth Shippen Green (1871–1954), who started as a fashion illustrator, went on to a forty-year career with *Harper's* while also illustrating numerous books.

The reverence of Pyle's students for their Chadds Ford experience was often expressed by anecdote. Frank Schoonover (1877–1972) remembered a fall day gathering nuts. Many had fallen into a stream, so Pyle and his students pulled off their shoes and socks and waded in. "When we came out of the water, we were shivering," said Schoonover, "and I remember Mr. Pyle said, 'That is the sort of feeling you must put into your work. That is the way the soldiers felt at Valley Forge. They felt that same chill. When you make an illustration of Valley Forge, that is the sort of thing that you must put into the picture.'"

Schoonover went on to fame as an illustrator of outdoor adventure stories for *Scribner's*, *Century*, *McClure's* and other magazines. In 1903, he spent four months exploring 1,200 miles of eastern Canadian wilderness by foot and dog sled for a series of illustrated stories that ran in 1905. Famous authors whose stories and books he illustrated include Edgar Rice Burroughs, Rex Beach, Zane Grey and Clarence Mulford (author of the *Hopalong Cassidy* stories).

Schoonover was also one of several Pyle alums to document World War I. Among his work was *Belleau Wood*, which depicts a June 1918 battle in which more than 1,800 Americans died to stop a German advance on Paris. The Battle of Belleau Wood was old-fashioned, up-close combat. In Schoonover's painting, U.S. foot soldiers are overwhelming an enemy trench. One of the Germans lies dead, another has thrown up his hands in surrender and a third is scrambling to get away. At the right, a Marine seems to have thrust his bayonet into a German's throat. At the center, a U.S. soldier's rifle is inches from the chest of another German who is strangely immobile; the man's chin seems to have dropped and his shoulders are hunched. Meanwhile, his hands are clenched as if...well, as if he has just stepped into a stream of cold water.

If this scene was on videotape, it would never be seen on U.S. television. Still, this is Pyle's legacy. And can't you just feel it?

1901: R. Brognard Okie and the McMansion Craze

Americans at the turn of the twenty-first century made fun of McMansions. But they were popular for lots of sensible reasons: They offered space. They were new. And they were stuffed with the gadgets and conveniences that affluent Americans loved. But there was another reason for their popularity, and it involved architects like R. Brognard Okie (1875–1945) of Newtown Square.

Most McMansions were just another twist on traditional architectural themes, of which Okie was one of the best-known and most-skilled practitioners. In addition to high-end residences for affluent clients, Okie restored landmarks such as the Betsy Ross house and, more locally, St. David's Church.

In Erie, Pennsylvania, Okie built a miniature of St. David's for a client who wanted a chapel on his estate. Okie reconstructions include Pennsbury Manor, William Penn's estate in Bucks County and "High Street," a recreation of colonial Market Street for the Philadelphia Sesquicentennial in 1926.

Perhaps Okie and his peers did their jobs too well. Americans fell in love with the Colonial style—previously considered passé—but most couldn't afford the authentic workmanship, materials and careful design that Okie's high-end clients demanded. Instead, most settled for mass-market versions that suggested the same look.

A startling example of this can still be seen at Okie's former residence, Hillside Farm, which he purchased in 1901. The one-hundred-acre estate came with an eighteenth-century stone farmhouse, to which Okie added a large servants' wing and many of the distinctive touches typically seen in his clients' houses. Since the mid-1990s, Berwyn Estates, a McMansion development, has surrounded the house.

McMansion popularity perplexed Okie's granddaughter, Penny McLain, an artist who inherited the property. "They have faux dormers," said McLain, who remembers watching in amazement as workers tacked prefabricated dormers to the new homes' plywood roofs.

But Colonial Revival was always about nostalgia, not function. The style was inspired by the 1876 Philadelphia Centennial, which brought fresh attention to the houses of the Founding Fathers. Architects tired of Victorian gingerbread began studying pre-Revolutionary houses and, soon, copied them nationwide. Colonial Revival was the dominant house style from about 1900 through the 1940s.

Originally, Colonial Revival houses were formal and symmetrical, with doors in the middle and equal numbers of windows on either side. Common features include Palladian windows, heavy moldings and porches with

Surrounded by tract houses in Newtown Square, Hillside—the eighteenth-century farmhouse that architect R. Brognard Okie rebuilt in his own faux Colonial style—is a forerunner of the housing trends that made McMansions popular. *Courtesy of Mark E. Dixon.*

classical columns. Fanlights or pediments topped elaborately paneled doors. Windows were double-hung. Paint colors were usually the chaste white or light yellows of the Federal era.

In southeastern Pennsylvania, Revival houses were often brick or stone. Many were designed to mimic old farmhouses that had grown by a series of additions. Mastering these forms and materials was where Okie excelled.

Today, tract developers are more likely to use Colonial elements as seasoning: a little molding here, a Palladian window there. Stoops are more common than porches, though they often come with (vinyl) Doric columns. And stone façades are often covered with lightweight imitation rocks manufactured with a flat side for easy gluing.

Okie, the son of a physician, was born in Camden. He studied mechanical engineering at Haverford College and graduated from the University of Pennsylvania in 1897 with a degree in architecture. After several years as an associate with a small firm, he went into partnership with Charles Ziegler, a restoration architect known for his involvement in the restorations of Carpenters Hall, Independence Hall and Washington's Headquarters at Valley Forge.

Ziegler and Okie worked together for nearly twenty years, after which Okie continued in independent practice for clients clustered heavily on the Main Line. Among them were Lewis and Anabel Parsons, who, in the 1920s, hired Okie to enlarge and renovate Appleford, their 1728 estate in Villanova. Appleford now belongs to Lower Merion Township, which rents it for special events.

What's notable about Appleford, according to architectural historian Jim Garrison, is how well Okie made its new parts look as old as its old parts. "Okie was very skilled in working in new pieces with the old, creating a seamless whole that had the total appearance of antiquity," said Garrison, a senior architect with the Hillier Group in Philadelphia.

At Appleford, rooms are gracious yet "chaste…with few concessions to modernity." Garrison also described Okie's work as "shy and retiring," yet McLain said that her grandfather once quit a job when the client refused to use the style of fence picket that he recommended.

Okie's favored materials were random rubble stone walls, wide board floors, hand-split cypress shingles and antique hardware. And his favored clients were rich. An old Chester County Day brochure describes Okie's "splendid" working relationship with Joseph Hergesheimer, who hired Okie to restore Dower House, a 1712 home near West Chester: "Both generously endowed with a passion for detail...they restored the old house correctly, without being too much swayed by cost."

Nearly sixty years after his death, Okie houses retain their appeal. "If I had an Okie listing, it would definitely the first thing I would mention to a buyer," said Barbara McClure of Remax Town & Country. "Most people who grew up here know the name." If they don't, she said, a good realtor would mention historical authenticity, quality interior woodwork and understated "classy" designs that make sense without being tricked up. "An Okie house is a good thing," said McClure.

At Hillside, Okie rebuilt the farmhouse to suit his own artistic vision and to serve as a 3-D brochure for clients. He knocked off a large dormer that he considered wrong for the structure and replaced it with a smaller version that matched two others.

Inside, Okie made extensive use of built-in cabinetry to hide twentieth-century intrusions. A key cabinet is behind a panel in the central hall. Under the stairs are cubbyholes for shoes. A baseboard panel opens to reveal a heating vent, but instead of a metal vent cover, warm air rises through a screen of turned spindles. Panels in the deep windowsills lift to reveal built-in window boxes. Wrought-iron hinges are faithful reproductions of those used in the colonial era.

McLain also pointed out a removable wood panel that allows the living room and library to be thrown together into one large room for crowds. It acknowledges that large spaces are sometimes useful but maintains the understanding that barn living is for animals.

Of all modern technology, Okie particularly disliked the automobile. Not once did he attach a garage to his new or restored homes, nor did he ever own a car himself. Instead, Okie commuted to his Philadelphia office by horse. According to McLain, her grandfather rode up Waterloo Road to the Devon train station where, as recently as the 1940s, an attendant was available to care for horses during the day. Ironically, Okie was killed when a drunk driver struck the car in which he was riding on West Chester Pike at Route 926.

McLain inherited the house from her late father, Charles, an architect who tried to follow in his father's footsteps, though less successfully. To help support his family, Charles Okie sold off the farm in pieces that were eventually acquired by a developer.

McLain reported little contact with development residents, whom she found strangely different. Once, when a barn burned on a neighboring property, residents of Berwyn Estates gathered in a cul-de-sac on a nearby hilltop, passed cups of coffee and had an impromptu party as they watched the blaze. McLain stayed inside and wept. "That barn was two hundred years old and it was just a real shame," she said.

But that, too, is part of the legacy of R. Brognard Okie. Skilled at creating high-quality fakes, he unwittingly helped stimulate a desire for cheap fakes. Three generations later, one result of all that fakery is that fewer people understand or appreciate the difference.

1911: Eddystone, Gateway to Sri Lanka

Your cellphone is made in China. Your sneakers come from Vietnam. And the workers in your ISP's call center are all in India. Jobs, it seems, are all going away. But that's not new. They're only going *farther* away.

Locally, business leaders have recognized since the early twentieth century that workers are easier to control—and work for less—in scattered suburban, even rural, facilities. Then, it wasn't necessary to go to Sri Lanka; Delaware County was fine. The point was to get out of Philadelphia, which offered too many opportunities to rub elbows with too many people who had way, way too many ideas.

A pioneer of the new feudalism was Baldwin Locomotive. In 1911, Baldwin CEO Samuel Vauclain (1856–1940) of Radnor used the company's then-new plant in Eddystone to bust the unions that had organized many of the ten thousand workers at its factory at Broad and Spring Garden Streets. When the suburban workers did not support their Center City brothers, Baldwin turned what had been intended as an addition to the Philadelphia facility into its replacement. Other industrialists soon followed this example. Ironically, Baldwin's flight to the suburbs did not save the company, whose failure in the 1950s has been attributed, in part, to its labor practices.

Anything Baldwin did got noticed. At the turn of the twentieth century, Baldwin Locomotive was the largest company in the world. It employed more than eighteen thousand people at its peak in 1907 and, during its 125-year (1831–1956) history, produced more than seventy-six thousand locomotives, most powered by steam. The company was founded by Matthias Baldwin (1795–1866), a Philadelphia machinist who built his first

A phalanx of Philadelphia police march past Baldwin Locomotive in the city's Spring Garden section in 1910. A violent strike that year convinced Baldwin officials to re-imagine the company's expansion to Eddystone into an abandonment of its Center City site. *Courtesy of Library of Congress.*

locomotive—a working model called "Old Ironsides"—without having ever seen a functioning locomotive himself. The company struggled until the Civil War, when military needs accelerated demand for new engines. Baldwin sold more than one hundred locomotives to the Pennsylvania Railroad alone. By the end of the war, the company's position within its industry was secure.

Baldwin Locomotive bought 184 acres for its Eddystone expansion in 1906. But the story of its exodus from Philadelphia really begins with a riot that grew out of the 1910 Philadelphia streetcar strike. Philadelphia police supported the management of the Philadelphia Rapid Transit Co. (PRT) with tactics that enraged not only the striking transit workers but also workers outside the industry and bystanders. Add PRT's corruption and unpopularity to the widely acknowledged miserable conditions in which the streetcar men worked, and the result was a citywide pro-union mood that was a boon for organizers in all industries.

On February 19, 1910, PRT strikers gathered at powerhouses in Kensington, Germantown and near the Baldwin plant. Workers from nearby factories joined the agitation, and the police were called out to protect company property. In Kensington, textile workers left their mills to block

Employees of Baldwin Locomotive gather in 1910 in front of the company's Spring Garden factory. During a violent strike that year, police fired at least two hundred shots into the plant, while workers responded by throwing nuts, bolts and other locomotive parts. *Courtesy of Library of Congress.*

tracks, blockade PRT powerhouses, smash streetcar windows and throw rocks at police and scabs. In Germantown, ten thousand sympathy strikers battled police for two hours, according to historian Ken Fones-Wolf. "Employers were faced with deciding how to respond when their workers were caught up in this generalized unrest," wrote Fones-Wolf. "Some pressured the city and the PRT to make concessions."

On February 23, mounted police responded when strikers again gathered near the Baldwin works. At midday, the police confronted the strikers, apparently in an effort to protect trolleys running up and down Broad Street. In doing so, they also clashed with Baldwin employees who had stopped on their lunch break to boo the men in blue. The police responded by firing on the Baldwin workers, wounding one in the leg. The uproar drew more Baldwin men outside.

William Austin, a Baldwin vice-president, described what happened next:

> *The police ran the men back into the shop and then trouble began. Before anyone knew what started it we heard pistol shots. I looked out of the office window and saw a long line of policemen, about two dozen, lined*

up in front of the Willow Street shop actually firing into the second and third story shop windows. They were answered by a volley of nuts, bolts, washers, shaft hangers, iron rods, etc., some very heavy, and all calculated to kill if landed in the right spot. The police shot at least 200 shots into the shops. Fortunately, no one was hurt on either side but for a while it was very serious business.

A foreman, J.L. Kimball, protested to a police sergeant about the use of firearms. "The sergeant whom we approached informed me that the police were shooting blank cartridges," he reported, "but the evidence of lead on the bricks and small holes in window panes proved otherwise." Newspapers around the country ran stories with large photos of what the *Duluth* (Minnesota) *News Tribune* headlined as the "Battle of the Baldwin Works."

Furious at what the *Philadelphia Bulletin* termed "Russian rule," the Central Labor Union—an umbrella group for organized labor in Philadelphia—called a citywide general strike on March 4 against all industries to support the streetcar workers. By the second day, more than 100,000 workers were on the street.

Baldwin workers were generally well paid, so Vauclain was genuinely surprised when many joined the strike. According to Fones-Wolf, the anti-management agitation had led employees to feel more than usually aggrieved over Baldwin's labor practices and determined to change them.

At Baldwin, skilled craftsmen were treated as quasi-independent contractors who bid on work, organized production and distributed earnings. "This system allowed contractors substantial earnings," wrote Fones-Wolf, "but it also encouraged favoritism in awarding contracts and it encouraged contractors to exploit their crews." The system also frustrated union organizing by making craftsmen, usually the backbone of trade unionism, hostile to organized labor. Other complaints—no overtime pay and low piecework rates—were related to the contracting system. By March 8, about one-third of Baldwin workers were on the picket line.

Vauclain, though, was not about to tolerate unions in his factory. The son of a Pennsylvania Railroad foreman who had previously worked for Matthias Baldwin, he had joined his father's shop at the age of sixteen. After a five-year apprenticeship, Vauclain moved to Philadelphia, where he went to work for Baldwin, becoming foreman of its Seventeenth Street shop in 1883, plant superintendent in 1886 and partner in 1896. He personally designed the "Vauclain Compound" locomotive, a four-cylinder locomotive that conserved fuel and water and operated more efficiently than anything previously made. According to Baldwin historian John K. Brown, Vauclain identified with workingmen and believed that he knew their concerns.

"Business advantage motivated his abhorrence of unions," wrote Brown, "[but] he sincerely believed in the virtues of individual effort, initiative and personal advancement, and he saw organized labor as antithetical to those principles."

At the time of the strike, Baldwin was preparing to raise money for expansion with a $10 million sale of bonds. Labor strife would hurt sales and would also interfere with the company's ability to fill orders, which were beginning to flood in again after a brief recession.

So Vauclain played it cool. He stated publicly that there would be no recriminations against strikers. He also granted workers a half-holiday on Saturdays—normally a regular workday—and even interceded on behalf of one worker who had been arrested at a demonstration. Finally, Vauclain announced that Baldwin was backlogged with orders and would hire an additional four thousand men to supplement its workforce.

"It is time," Vauclain told the *Public Ledger* newspaper, that "we are taking advantage of [prosperity] by forgetting there is such a thing as a strike." This response won Baldwin and Vauclain much praise from both the press and other employers. Even "Mrs. R.A.C.," a worker's wife, wrote in with her thanks: "It is only Christian people with good characters who make the smallest bow to a humble workman and I believe you must be this kind of a man."

Meanwhile, Vauclain was sending spies into union meetings to identify dissatisfied workers. Vauclain's papers at the Historical Society of Pennsylvania include a handwritten report by an unnamed spy who described "a few short talks by different speakers of whom some were men from our shop. I do not know them [nor] could I ascertain their names but their faces were familiar." In addition, the spy reported, "Capital was abused...and, in fact, it was as near an anarchist meeting as could be."

At the same time, work continued at the new Eddystone plant. The facility had been planned for several years after it became apparent that the old downtown shops were too small to produce the increasingly large modern locomotives. In some cases, Baldwin had to knock down walls to get the new machines out of its shops. Now, though, Eddystone would be useful in a new way.

In the spring of 1911, Baldwin began to transfer to Delaware County carloads of workers—especially younger workers who had few attachments to unions. At the same time, it completed the orders that had led it to expand the workforce the previous year and announced eight thousand layoffs, most from the downtown plant. Union men went first, according to muckraking journalist John Reed, who wrote, "The first to be discharged were the members of [union] committees, who were cynically told that this was the chance their employers had been waiting for."

The layoffs produced another large strike. Prominent labor agitators came to demonstrate and, in fact, kept the strike going for several months. But the Eddystone workers never responded. Baldwin was thus able to continue production and break the unions' effectiveness. With competition fierce for the remaining jobs, Baldwin workers gave up. At Eddystone, foremen demanded that all workers entering the plant tear up their union papers and deliver them to the plant superintendent.

By 1928, Baldwin had moved its entire operation to Eddystone. The old red brick structures in North Philadelphia were demolished in 1937. Baldwin, which later failed to make a successful transition to the production of diesel locomotives, stopped production in 1956.

The long-term consequences were profound: by the early twenty-first century, the United States had mostly forgotten how to build locomotives. When federal officials began planning a network of high-speed trains, the only qualified suppliers were in France, Spain, Germany and Canada. See what a move to Eddystone can start?

1915: Anna and the Tax Man

We live at the mercy of petty officials. Legislatures, presidents and courts have their places. But the *real* power to make our lives hell lies in the anonymous ranks of cops, zoning officers, tax officials and clerks.

Suffragist Anna Howard Shaw (1847–1919), for instance, was the nation's top suffragist from 1905 to 1915, when she led the National American Woman Suffrage Association (NAWSA). She was on a first-name basis with the national leaders of her day. But it was a lowly Upper Providence Township tax assessor who, in 1915, confiscated and sold Shaw's yellow roadster.

Shaw claimed to be resisting an unjust tax. She owned a house in Moylan, which, in the view of Delaware County, made her a local resident and liable for a tax on personal property. But Shaw refused to complete a form listing her assets. It was "heaping injury upon tyranny," she told the *New York Times*, that someone forbidden to vote was required to list property to be taxed without representation. "In the spirit of 1776," said Shaw, "I decline to be a party to an act which violates the national Constitution."

Born in England, Shaw was the daughter of a Scottish grain merchant. In earlier generations, the Shaws had been Highland landowners with their own castle, and Anna grew up hearing how her ancestors had resisted the Romans, the British and other clans. "It gives me no pleasure to read the grisly details of their struggles," she wrote in her 1915 autobiography, "but I confess to a certain satisfaction that my ancestors made a good showing in the defense of what was theirs."

In 1851, after her father's bankruptcy, the Shaws sailed for America— "the great dream of those days"—and settled in Massachusetts, where her

Anna Howard Shaw (left) was the nation's top suffragist from 1904 to 1915, when she headed the National American Woman's Suffrage Association. But that didn't stop a Delaware County tax official from seizing and auctioning her car for unpaid taxes. *Courtesy of Library of Congress.*

father worked in a shipyard. The Shaws were Unitarian and progressive. Attracted to abolition, they rubbed shoulders with leaders of that movement, including Robert Gould Shaw (no relation), who would die leading an African American regiment in the Civil War.

In 1859, Thomas Shaw sent his family west to farm 360 acres he had purchased in northern Michigan. (He remained working in Massachusetts for another year.) The property included a dirt-floor cabin, into which both animals and the local Ottawa Indians ventured at will. Shaw's mother, who expected a tidy English farm, was horrified. Years later, Shaw believed her father irresponsible for putting them in that situation.

"Like most men, my dear father should never have married," she wrote. "He gave no thought to the manner in which we were to make the struggle and survive the hardships before us." Shaw's father, she wrote, was the sort to spend planting season calculating the average number of corn kernels per ear rather than getting it planted.

In 1862, Thomas Shaw and his two sons all responded to news of Fort Sumter by enlisting in a Michigan cavalry regiment. They didn't return until 1865. "Between those years, I was the principal support of our family," wrote Shaw, who had begun teaching school for two dollars per week at the age of fifteen. Her mother took in sewing, the women made and sold quilts and they took in boarders.

After the war, Shaw moved in with a married sister in Big Rapids, Michigan, and attended high school. She became active in the Methodist church, preaching her first sermon when she was twenty-three and being licensed to preach a year later. In 1873, she entered Albion College, paying for her two years' of education there by preaching and lecturing on temperance. In 1876, she left Albion to attend Boston Theological Seminary, where she was the only woman in her class. Upon graduation in 1878, she took charge of a church in East Dennis, Massachusetts.

In East Dennis, Shaw personally faced down a group of unbelievers who had invaded her church's Christmas celebration and threatened to dance—something forbidden among Methodists. Though not personally opposed to dancing, Shaw was determined to uphold Methodist order. "Every man and woman who interrupts our exercises by attempting to dance, or by creating a disturbance of any kind, will be arrested tomorrow morning," she announced from the center of the floor. Meanwhile, rather than back her up, the Methodist men disappeared out the doors.

And, she said, "I will have the women arrested first!" That settled it. None of the women dared dance, and none of the men cared to dance alone. Shaw waited out the invaders until midnight, the legal closing time, when they finally dispersed.

But Shaw was only a probationary minister. And, in 1880, when her ordination came before the General Conference of the Methodist Episcopal Church, it was refused because she was a woman. The church also sought to revoke her preaching license. Shaw turned to the Methodist Protestant Church, a separate denomination, for ordination so she could continue her ministry.

In 1882, "after I had been in East Dennis four years, I began to feel I was getting into a rut," Shaw later wrote. And "because I realized the splendid work women could do as physicians, I began to study medicine." While continuing to serve her churches, she commuted to Boston Medical School, obtaining a diploma in 1885.

Shaw never practiced medicine. During her studies, she met suffragist Lucy Stone and Stone's husband, Harry Blackwell, brother of Elizabeth

Blackwell, the first U.S. female physician. "Together," wrote Shaw, "they developed in me a vital interest in the suffrage cause, which grew steadily from that time until it became the dominating influence in my life."

Shaw resigned her pastorates and became a lecturer for the Massachusetts Woman's Suffrage Association. From 1886 to 1892, she headed the suffrage efforts of the Women's Christian Temperance Union, which believed that women's votes would lead to the banning of alcohol.

Shaw became close to Susan B. Anthony, who had served as president of NAWSA since 1890, when she led the merger of two earlier organizations. Shaw succeeded "Aunt Susan" in 1904 and was at the older woman's bedside when she died two years later. According to Shaw, Anthony died with these words: "Promise me that you will keep the presidency of the association as long as you are well enough to do the work." And Shaw agreed.

Suffrage historians credit Shaw as a stirring speaker with a sharp wit. On the stump, she liked to tell stories about encounters with opponents, like the man who insisted women had never produced anything of value to the world. "I told him," responded Shaw, "that the chief product of the women had been the men, and left it to him to decide whether the product was of any value." After she spoke at Bryn Mawr College in 1914, sophomore Helen Robertson described Shaw in a letter as "sharp as a needle."

On the other hand, Shaw has not been remembered as an effective leader. There were few suffrage victories on her watch, and the movement splintered over tactics. Shaw condemned as disrespectful the picketing of the Wilson White House by Alice Paul and other suffragists. And Shaw's needle-like tongue did make enemies. Most significantly, suffrage passed *after* she was replaced by Carrie Chapman Catt, who introduced a more aggressive strategy.

Shaw came to Moylan in 1908. For most of her career, she had lived in rented quarters or as someone's guest. But she had longed, wrote Shaw, "to build on a tract which had a stream, a grove of trees, great boulders and rocks and a hill site for the house with a broad outlook." A lot on Rose Valley Road, a block from the train station, sufficed.

Moylan borders Rose Valley, founded by freethinkers as a single-tax, arts-and-crafts paradise. The community was popular with artists and intellectuals who would have been sympathetic to suffrage. Shaw had chosen a friendly community.

Well, except for the tax man.

In 1914, Shaw had fallen and broken her ankle getting off a train in Jersey City. Her supporters' gift—reported in all the papers—of a yellow roadster in June 1915 was probably an effort to help her get around more easily. Yellow was the color of the suffrage movement, and in an era in which all cars were black, the vehicle attracted attention wherever it went. Shaw named it "Eastern Victory" and took a brief vacation to learn how to drive.

Shaw's dispute with assessor Louis Little began in 1914, when he first requested that she list her property so that he could calculate her tax. Assessments ranged from $1.20 to $6.00 per person. Shaw told Little that she considered herself a resident of New York, where NAWSA was headquartered. Little took no notice of this, and Shaw later claimed that he had boasted before witnesses that he "would make the assessment so large she would be compelled to make out the statement." Little's assessment was $30,000—at a time when $3,000 would buy a large house. The tax due: $126.

On July 12, two weeks after Shaw received the car, Little and Constable A.C.W. Mathues found her garage unlocked. Matthues backed out "Eastern Victory" and drove it into Media, where he locked it in Pierson's Garage. According to the *Philadelphia Inquirer*, "The course taken by the constable ran him by the headquarters of the suffrage party of the county, and a number of women there gazed on what they considered almost a sacrilege."

Appeals to Little, the county commissioners and a local court were ignored. Shaw—whose lifelong disappointment with men began with her father—undoubtedly considered this just more male bullying. She told reporters she would never pay. But Shaw's friends intervened. When the car went to auction July 24, suffrage supporters bought and returned it, though anti-suffrage bidders pushed the price from $126 to $230.

Would she have been so treated, Shaw asked a Norristown audience later that month, "if I had been a voter in Delaware County, an influential member of the community, one of the electorate to whom judges must appeal for votes?"

Well, would she? As anyone—male or female—knows who has faced an indifferent clerk: yes, probably.

1917: Tiptoe around the Powerful

Never make politicians look stupid. Vote against them if you want. But reveal them to voters as incompetent and they'll come after you.

As an example, consider all those who, between 1917 and 1939, made it a top priority to capture and punish a German brewer's son who didn't want to go to war. Unfortunate mostly for himself, Grover Cleveland Bergdoll (1893–1966) successfully dodged the draft for all those years while federal officials held hearings, postured and fumed—and mostly ignored thousands of other draft dodgers.

Bergdoll was twenty-four when the ordeal began. When the public servants were finished with him, he was fifty-one.

"Bergdoll had insulted America!" said Corliss Hooven Griffis, who unsuccessfully tried to kidnap Bergdoll from his refuge in Germany in 1923. "It was every American's duty to punish him. German soldiers who fought against us may now be my friends. Cowards and traitors may never be."

Born in Philadelphia, Bergdoll was the grandson of a German immigrant who had founded a brewery here in 1846. At its height, the Louis Bergdoll Brewery at Twenty-ninth and Girard Streets supplied more than 1,400 saloons and taverns.

All that beer supported a lavish lifestyle, which included sending Louis Jr. back to the Fatherland for a German bride: Emma Barth of Bavaria. Louis Sr. died in 1894 and Louis Jr. only two years later, leaving Emma with five children and the business.

Grover was Emma's third child, named for the then-sitting twenty-fourth president. Emma later claimed to admire Grover Cleveland for avoiding military service during the Civil War by paying a substitute.

The family of Grover Cleveland Bergdoll—including his mother, Emma, seated at right—waited in a U.S. Senate bathroom in 1939 as their lawyer announced that Bergdoll would surrender the next day on twenty-two-year-old charges of draft evasion. *Courtesy of Library of Congress.*

None of the Bergdoll children got much supervision. Emma was busy managing the brewery and other business holdings. According to historian Roberta E. Dell, she regularly worked on her books until midnight. "I did not have much time to bother about [Grover's adolescence]," Emma would later say. "I had to take care of everything, look after the properties, rents and so on."

Grover, though, had a blast. In 1912, at age eighteen, he bought a Wright biplane and, wrote Dell, "terrorized" the community—panicking horses, dive-bombing rooftops, racing trains and chasing bathers at the Jersey Shore. (The plane is now at the Franklin Institute.)

Grover and his brother, Erwin, both spent thousands on racing cars, which they raced on city streets by day and tinkered with at night. "Speeding tickets, arrests, accidents and complaints soon became synonymous with the name Bergdoll," wrote Dell.

In 1915, Grover turned twenty-one and came into a million-dollar inheritance. He also moved into a stone house in Wynnefield purchased for him by his mother. Later, Erwin was gifted a turreted stone mansion in Broomall, located where the southbound Blue Route exits to West Chester Pike.

In June 1917, Grover registered for the draft, which he likely gave little thought. At home, he was busy building a balloon. The United States had declared war against Germany in April, and a mass mobilization was underway. Emma, however, was offended by the shrill anti-German propaganda. With little initial support for war, the Wilson administration offered overheated rhetoric about German barbarism. In the hysteria, high schools cancelled German classes. Beethoven was excised from concerts. Sauerkraut became Liberty Cabbage.

According to Dell, Emma considered the United States an aggressor against "her brave little country." Grover's relatives lived in Germany. Would he be required to shoot them?

Uncle Sam, rock. Mom, hard place.

In August, Grover disappeared. Vacation, he later claimed. Grover had a relatively high draft number so could have reasonably expected delay before being called. But when he returned in September, events had leaped forward. Grover's number had already been called. He hadn't reported, so he was now a wanted man.

(There remains some question as to why Grover's number was called. His lawyer would later charge that the head of his draft board—a neighbor whose children Grover had spanked when they climbed a special cherry tree—had illegally moved Grover's number up in the process to get even.)

Again, Grover disappeared. Disappearing had worked when he was wanted for speeding. Often, the Philadelphia police just forgot about everything. But the feds were different. And Grover's speeding raps had never unleashed the sort of fury now directed at what the newspapers called the "son of a German mother."

Anti-German prejudice has deep roots in America. Both Benjamin Franklin and John Adams grumbled over German colonists' lack of enthusiasm for the Revolution. One historian has estimated that 60 percent of German-descended colonists were either neutral or loyal to George III, himself of German descent.

In the nineteenth century, Germans—many Catholic—were targets of the anti-immigrant, anti-Catholic Know-Nothing movement, which later melted into the Republican Party. When the Civil War came, those

Grover Cleveland Bergdoll—seated, with goggles, in one of his airplanes—had no interest in World War I. But when he ignored a draft notice, his affluence and German background made him a handy political target. *Courtesy of Marple-Newtown Historical Society.*

German Catholics remembered who their enemies had been and were slow to sign on with the Union cause. After the Irish, Germans were the most underrepresented group in the Union army. "Opposition to [emancipation and the draft] was strongest among Irish and German Catholics," wrote Civil War historian James McPherson.

Before World War I, German Americans organized to challenge British influence. After the war, they turned en masse against Woodrow Wilson's Democrats. In scores of German-settled midwestern counties, Democrats' share of the vote fell 25 to 50 percent between 1916 and 1920. During the war, however, chasing a "German" draft dodger was good politics.

With Grover underground, the heat fell on Emma, who naïvely worsened her situation by offering to buy her son an exemption from the draft, as Cleveland had bought his. Naturally, draft officials reported this bribery attempt and the thick German accent in which it was made. Arrested and charged with helping Grover escape, Emma was finally released with a $200 fine.

Meanwhile, Erwin Bergdoll's draft number was called, and he joined Grover on the run. Well, "run." The pair wasn't very discreet, wrote Dell, dividing their time between a Maryland hotel and their homes in Wynnefield and Broomall. Frustrated by how he was portrayed, Grover vented in a letter to the *Philadelphia Ledger*, offering to turn himself in if allowed to serve as a flying instructor. "Your paper calls me a pro-German," he wrote. "That statement is an infamous lie and a rank falsehood."

Fugitive draft dodgers weren't supposed to talk back. So now the feds upped the ante, reclassifying Grover as a deserter. The message was clear: in wartime, deserters were shot.

After three years, the feds finally noticed that sightings of Grover peaked around the holidays. In January 1920, Grover and Erwin—home to spend Christmas and the New Year with Emma—were asleep in their respective houses. Emma had spent the night with Grover in Wynnefield. At dawn, Philadelphia police kicked in the door. Emma, grabbing a revolver and a blackjack, met the officers at the door, where she knocked one to the floor. Grover was found in a window seat.

Outside, "both men and women, wild eyed and tight lipped, screamed at him, calling him a traitor as he passed," wrote Dell of the mob that had gathered on Grover's lawn. "Others cursed him and his entire family."

Erwin escaped but later turned himself in.

Sentenced to five years, Grover then produced a story about $150,000 in gold buried in Virginia. He worried that it would be gone when he got out. Strangely, military authorities allowed him out with two guards to dig it up. During a brief stop at his mother's house, Grover stepped away—supposedly to answer a phone—and escaped in his own car, which was conveniently parked outside. Eventually, he crossed into Canada and sailed for Germany.

Congress subsequently convened a committee to investigate the escape, the Bergdoll gold and the family's "pro-Germanism." In the process, Representative Ben Johnson of Kentucky accused Grover's brother Charles of evasion. When Charles called Johnson a liar, the congressman pulled a revolver and started after him until restrained.

But Grover's troubles weren't over. In 1921, Grover's car was surrounded by six men wielding guns. Two U.S. soldiers and four hired Germans planned to carry Grover to U.S.-occupied territory. But Grover pushed away the man at the window, and his driver floored it in a hail of bullets. One shot wounded a woman in the back seat. Though arrested and convicted, the kidnappers were released after pressure from Washington. The secretary of state publicly vowed to "get Bergdoll." Grover cabled hopes for the secretary's funeral.

Next, Griffis and several hired men jumped Grover in his room. But Grover, who carried a gun, killed one assailant in the struggle. The rest were arrested and convicted and then pardoned after two million Americans signed petitions for their release. In New York, Griffis was welcomed with ticker tape.

In 1927, Grover married a German girl with whom he would have six children. In 1933, hoping to be included in Franklin Roosevelt's general amnesty for war offenders, Grover was disappointed to learn that the proclamation had been phrased to exclude him. U.S. politicians were still vengeful.

By 1939, Jewish and other refugees were fleeing Germany. Perhaps this gave a southern representative, Forest Harness, his sadistic idea. In April, Harness introduced legislation to revoke Grover's citizenship, thus barring him from the country. In effect, that would make him a prisoner in Nazi Germany.

"Do the rigors of the Hitler dictatorship chafe his wastrel, playboy soul?" Harness taunted from the House. The bill passed unanimously. Warned that it would likely pass the Senate in May, Grover opted to come home. If he was on U.S. soil first, the bill would be moot.

And that's how it happened. Seized at a New York pier, Grover went straight to Leavenworth, leaving his lawyer to release a public apology for the past twenty-two years. In it, Grover made sure to mention the Statue of Liberty, "which gloriously greets all the refugees coming to the United States."

To his surprise, Grover now received letters of support from friendly strangers. Perhaps his contrition had finally broken the spell of public anger. Or, as likely, his case had become old and our public servants had other issues to posture over.

1918: The Importance of Matching Shoes

Always dress appropriately. Sweats are fine for the gym but not so much for a wedding. A bikini (or less) is okay for a French beach, but not if the beach is in Iran.

Boxer Jack Dempsey (1895–1983) learned this lesson the hard way. In 1918—the year before he became heavyweight champion of the world—he posed for publicity photos at Sun Ship in Chester wearing overalls and patent leather shoes.

Dempsey's stated intention that day was to encourage workers to take jobs in defense plants. But the contrast between his overalls and his shoes made it obvious that he was no shipyard worker. And that raised questions about why a guy who lived by combat wasn't in the army. Which, combined with damning words from his estranged ex-wife, eventually led to his indictment and trial for draft evasion.

"Dempsey, 6-feet-1 of strength in the glowing splendor of his youth, a man fashioned by nature as an athlete and a warrior...did not go to the war while weak-armed, strong-hearted clerks reeled under pack and rifle," sneered the *New York Times*. "Our greatest fighter sidestepped our greatest fight."

The episode nearly destroyed Dempsey's career.

Born in a log cabin in Manassa, Colorado, William Harrison "Harry" Dempsey was the ninth of eleven children. His parents, Hyrum and Celia, had traveled there in a covered wagon from West Virginia, where they were converted by a Mormon missionary who also told them of wonderful possibilities in the mountain states. But the possibilities were never realized for Hyrum, who spent his life as a day laborer.

During World War I, bustling Sun Ship seemed the perfect place for boxer Jack Dempsey to toss on a pair of overalls and pretend to help out. But his PR person didn't notice the contrast between the overalls and Dempsey's patent-leather shoes. Dempsey was widely ridiculed. *Courtesy of Delawarecountyhistory.com.*

Manassa was a scrappy sort of town surrounded by ranches and silver mines. Its rough-and-tumble workers enjoyed a good fight. Dempsey and his brothers picked up the ethos. And because of their Irish last name, they competed with each other for the nickname "Jack." An earlier and unrelated—but also Irish—Jack Dempsey (1862–1895) had held the middleweight title from 1884 to 1891. Dubbed "The Nonpareil" for his excellence in the ring, he'd been memorialized with a somber poem, "The Nonpareil's Grave," lamenting his early death and unmarked resting place:

> *'Tis strange New York should thus forget*
> *its bravest of the brave*
> *and in the wilds of Oregon*
> *unmarked, leave Dempsey's grave.*

"My brothers and I all knew that poem," the later Dempsey recalled. "All of us wanted to be the new Jack Dempsey." So when Harry Dempsey turned out to be the best fighter in Manassa, he also won the right to be "Jack."

In 1911, after finishing the eighth grade, Dempsey quit school and left home. For five years, he lived on the road. He took any kind of job, from washing dishes and scrubbing floors to mining coal and picking fruit. And when he couldn't get work, he begged for food and hopped railroad cars. A photograph of Dempsey from this period revealed a face, observed one biographer, on which were written his reasons for leaving home. "The nose, broken in several places, the expressionless mouth, and the cold haunting eyes suggest a childhood that had been less than kind," wrote biographer Randy Roberts.

Dempsey also began to fight as a source of income. Calling himself "Kid Blackie," he fought an estimated one hundred fights in Colorado, Utah and Nevada by mid-1914. Sometimes he lost because, as Roberts wrote, "in the world of miners, cowboys, railroad workers and lumberjacks, there was frequently someone who could maul a 130-pound 16-year-old."

But often he won. In Nevada, he once walked from Tonopah to Goldfield in the desert heat of July to fight a fellow known as "One-Punch Hancock" for his ability to put opponents on the floor quickly. The fight was in the back room of a bar. Fifteen seconds into the fight, Dempsey knocked out Hancock with one punch. The purse was five dollars.

In 1916, Dempsey found his first serious manager. By then, he'd beaten all serious fighters in the Rocky Mountain states. So the pair used what money they had to buy train tickets to New York, where they slept in Central Park. In July, Dempsey beat a well-known local fighter, "Wild Bert" Kenny, in ten hard-hitting rounds, winning fourteen rounds and the attention of local sportswriters—including the influential Damon Runyan.

Publicity brought him to the attention of John Reisler, a Manhattan fight promoter. Reisler got rid of Dempsey's manager by sending the man a fake telegram that his mother was sick. Taking over Dempsey's career, Reisler set up a fight with black boxer John Lester Johnson at the Harlem Sporting Club. Johnson broke three of Dempsey's ribs in the second round, but Dempsey fought back for the entire ten-round match. Johnson won the decision, but Dempsey won the crowd's cheers and $170, of which his new manager took $135. "This comes out to 10 bucks for each broken rib and two-fifty for each black eye," thought Dempsey.

Disgusted, the fighter rode a freight home, took a job shoveling in a copper mine and, in October 1916, married a prostitute named Maxine Cates, who also played piano at Maxim's, a Salt Lake City saloon. Years later, Dempsey remembered that "something like electricity" ran through him when Cates leaned forward in a revealing dress and said, "Hi, stranger. I'm Maxine from Maxim's. Who are you?" He was nineteen; she was thirty-five. The couple grew apart within a year. Dempsey was away, fighting and looking for fights.

Maxine, who liked the fast life, drifted back to prostitution. The couple finally divorced in 1919.

In 1917, Dempsey met John "Doc Kearns" McKernan, the manager who would lift him to stardom. Kearns, a former welterweight, knew boxing. That spring, as the United States was preparing to enter World War I, Dempsey began a string of nine fights. He won them all. In 1918, he won twenty-one of twenty-two matches from Buffalo down to New Orleans. On eleven different occasions, he knocked out his opponent in the first round.

By 1919, Dempsey was the only logical choice to go up against heavyweight champion "Big Jess" Willard—who stood six feet, six inches tall and weighed 245 pounds. In 1915, Willard had won the title from Jack Johnson in a sweltering outdoor match at Havana. Johnson was black, so Willard was dubbed the "Great White Hope" for returning the title to the "white race." He defended the title twice in 1916, but championship matches were suspended during the war. After three years of inactivity, Willard was overly confident and poorly prepared.

Dempsey put the boxer down seven times in the first round. He broke Willard's jaw and cheekbone and knocked out several teeth. Willard was done after the third round. (View the fight, which was filmed, at Youtube.com.)

Dempsey was now the heavyweight champion. But he soon had problems.

In 1917, Dempsey had registered with the Selective Service, requesting 4-A classification as the sole support for his wife and mother. That exempted him from military service. How much support Dempsey provided would be disputed.

Draft avoidance was hardly unique. Babe Ruth enlisted in the Massachusetts National Guard but never missed a game. Huey Long was exempted for being a notary public, Conrad Aiken for his poetry and Edsel Ford for being an employee of Ford Motor Co.—all essential civilian activities.

In the super-heated patriotism of World War I, such tricks were scorned. In Manhattan, wrote Roberts, society women stopped men in civilian clothes to present them with white feathers, symbols of cowardice. Actual and suspected draft dodgers were beaten and jailed.

In the fall of 1918, Dempsey was still relatively unknown. But Kearns had great plans for his up-and-coming young fighter. Probably, he thought it a good idea to depict Dempsey as an active supporter of the war.

"In the shipyard," Dempsey later recalled, "I was given a pair of striped overalls and told to slip them on over my street clothes. Snap. Snap. Snap. And that was that. The next morning, I unfolded the newspaper, and there I was, dressed in those crisp overalls with my shiny patent-leather, suede-topped shoes sticking out like sore thumbs."

Kearns's PR stunt had backfired. Dempsey was now an example of what many scorned.

"Dempsey is the champion *boxer*, but not the champion fighter," wrote sportswriter Grantland Rice after the Dempsey-Willard fight. "It would be an insult to every young American who sleeps today from Flanders to Lorraine, from the Somme to the Argonne, to crown Dempsey with any laurels built of fighting courage."

This might have faded. But, by 1920, Cates was divorced, working in a brothel in Wells, Nevada, and jealous of Dempsey's new wealth and glory. She wrote the *San Francisco Chronicle* that Dempsey had lied to the Selective Service about supporting her. "To tell the truth, I had to support him," she wrote. Cates claimed to have letters in which Dempsey asked her to sign an affidavit that he had supported her so he could dodge the draft. She also said the heavyweight champion had broken her jaw in an argument in their hotel room.

Indicted within weeks, Dempsey would be acquitted in seven minutes. Cates couldn't produce the letters, and the defense showed that she had tried to extort $40,000 from Dempsey. Dempsey's elderly mother testified that she had received support, and the fighter produced receipts for money sent to Cates. A naval officer testified that Dempsey had tried to enlist, and other evidence showed that Dempsey had fought benefit matches that yielded nearly $300,000 for war relief. Against all of which there was only the testimony of Cates, an admitted prostitute who would die four years later in a brothel fire in Juarez, Mexico.

Dempsey could've married better, of course. But was the Sun Ship photographer in such a hurry that Dempsey couldn't have pulled on a pair of work boots?

1937: Preparing for Change

Do people prepare for change? Or, when it happens, do they simply learn to deal?

The 1937 admission of the first Negro student at Media Friends School (MFS)—the area's first Quaker school to integrate—suggests that a firm push is often necessary. (The school later merged with another to become Media-Providence Friends School.)

Many parents weren't ready. The school nearly collapsed when one-third removed their children. An inspired few enrolled children for the first time. And integration-minded Quakers learned that, while someone has to push for change, there are ways *not* to go about it.

"Integration elsewhere was much later—and much smoother, less dramatic and less costly to the financial health of the schools," wrote Sue Gold, a former teacher at Media–Providence Friends School. "But Media Friends had shown the way."

Founded in 1876, MFS's first class—twelve students and one teacher— met over a stable on Baltimore Pike. In 1881, the school was adopted by Media Quakers "for the accommodation of Friends' children and others who were willing to comply with our rules." In 1885, MFS built a one-story brick structure next door to the Quaker meetinghouse. Tuition was twenty-one dollars a year.

Though founded relatively late, MFS was similar to dozens of Quaker schools that dotted the region beginning in the colonial period. An educated population had been part of William Penn's vision. In his 1682 *Fundamental Laws of the Province of Pennsylvania*, Penn wrote that "all persons having children shall cause such to be instructed...so that they may be able to read the Scriptures and to write by the time they attain to 12 years of age." In the mid-eighteenth century, Friends also established schools for girls and for blacks.

Many of these schools went out of business with the arrival of free public education in the 1830s. Some turned over their buildings for the new schools' use. Others, particularly upper schools such as Friends Select (Philadelphia), Westtown (Chester County) and the George School (Newtown, Bucks County), became more peculiarly Quaker to differentiate themselves. That appealed to many Friends who, amid social change, thought their children more likely to remain in the faith if they didn't mix with non-Quakers. Other Quakers were skeptical of the generic Protestantism observed in public schools. Still others thought public schools too accepting of militarism and of an unquestioning type of patriotism.

MFS preserved some distinctive practices. Students attended meeting once a week and called the days and months by their number—"Second Day," for instance, rather than Monday. Quaker students used "thee" and "thou," but non-Quakers were excused from this practice.

Like private schools today, MFS attracted affluent professionals. A survey of fathers' professions in the late 1940s found three lawyers, two advertising writers, three farmers, a photographer and thirty-one engineers. The school itself, however, was not rich. There was no endowment. MFS paid teachers' salaries and overhead out of tuition. There wasn't much excess, and if fewer students enrolled than expected, there could be problems.

In 1934, in the depth of the Depression, the school advised its four teachers that they would have jobs "with the understanding that all revenue for the period after payment of operating expenses would be available for teachers' income." The teachers, also responsible for maintenance and fencing the play area, agreed. Fortunately, seventy-five students enrolled, generating enough revenue to pay everyone, plus a couple of part-timers. "The committee feels and desires that the meeting should share its deep sense of obligation to the teachers…for going ahead in the face of financial uncertainty," wrote T. Barclay Witson, chairman of the board.

One advantage of MFS's hand-to-mouth existence was that the board had little investment to protect. It could afford to take chances and, perhaps, exercise some principles.

In 1904, MFS had sponsored five Doukhobor children and a married couple who cared for them at a rented house in Media. The Doukhobors were Russian pacifists persecuted by the Czar who had immigrated to Saskatchewan. During the world wars, the school resisted demands that its students perform patriotic exercises. In 1921, at an annual community fair, MFS displayed student essays on the disarmament conference that followed

The desegregation of Media Friends School in 1937 was a bumpy business but showed other Quaker schools how to go about it. By the time these students were photographed in the 1950s, integration was no longer controversial. *Courtesy of Media–Providence Friends School.*

World War I. "This was one of the best ways in which the school could acquaint the general community with its unique philosophy," wrote former teacher Vincent Pinto in a 1976 centennial book.

MFS always had non-Quaker students. In 1950, a survey of students' religious affiliations found equal numbers of Quakers and Methodists (twenty each), followed by Episcopalians (twelve); Lutherans (nine); Presbyterians, Baptists and Jews (eight each); Unitarians (six); Catholics (four); and one Pentecostal. A 1932 brochure declared the school "open to children of all parents who are in sympathy with our ideals, regardless of religious affiliation." The brochure made no mention of race, but in fact, all students were white.

In January 1937, the chair of the school committee received a phone call. "This is Mrs. McKnight of Media, Dr. McKnight's wife," said a female voice. "I am wondering how the Media Friends School would feel about having our little boy in the nursery school?" Always eager for students of the right kind, the official said MFS would be "delighted."

"Would you really?" said the woman in a surprised tone. And only then did Dorothy Biddle James realize that she was speaking with a black woman.

Thelma McKnight was the wife of Lancess McKnight, MD, who maintained a medical practice in Media while also serving as physician at Cheyney University. (Cheyney's McKnight-Rogers Hall, dedicated in 1977, honors McKnight's nearly forty years of service.) Their son, Lancess Jr., was four years old.

There is no record that blacks had ever applied to MFS previously. But, in 1933, the Quaker Westtown School had rejected two sons of black activist Max Yergan, then working for the international YMCA. It ignored a recommendation from the president of Fisk University who called Yergan "one of the most influential Christian statesman of the world today." A poll of Westtown parents revealed most so opposed to integration that they would withdraw their children. Some responses were openly racist.

Historically, nearly all American and European Quakers have been white. And Quakers don't proselytize, so they have mostly remained white. Some Quakers had been leaders in the antislavery and civil rights movements, but the rank and file had never been immune to prejudice.

Even the most progressive Friends preferred a white-glove approach to work on behalf of the Negro. In 1930, Philadelphia Quakers' race relations committee wrote to President Hoover, protesting his appointment of known racist John J. Parker to the Supreme Court. The group also lobbied Harrisburg to require insurers to write auto insurance policies for blacks, who often had trouble getting coverage.

But mixing with blacks was another matter, as Sadie T.M. Alexander complained to the committee in 1938. Alexander, the first black woman admitted to the Pennsylvania bar, was upset that blacks had been turned away from Friends Hospital and her own daughter from Germantown Friends School. "This refusal," wrote Alexander, "brings before my eyes and those of other concerned Negro people the question as to the real attitude of the Society of Friends toward the Negro people of America."

James visited the McKnights that evening. They didn't want trouble. "All I want," said Lancess McKnight, "is the best for my child just as you want the best for yours." James recommended acceptance. The committee concurred and decided to move ahead with no announcement to parents. "Had a white child applied in the middle of the year, no letter would be sent," James later wrote.

Little Lancess arrived on a Monday in mid-February. Protest erupted on Thursday, culminating in a Sunday gathering at which thirty-nine dissenting parents signed a letter informing the school they would not "be preached to." "If, after the end of the current school year," said the letter, "you continue to have as a pupil a child who is a Negro, we fear that it will be inadvisable for us to continue to send our children to the school." Other letters—including some from respected Quakers—warned that most Negroes carried venereal disease. The children, too.

Even some of the Media Quakers who officially controlled the school were critical. But they declined to interfere. Therefore, wrote James, "the committee felt it right to proceed." It told parents that the decision would stand. "We feel it right," wrote James, "to uphold the principle of treating applicants as individuals and not to exclude a colored person as such."

School opened that fall with sixty-two children, down from ninety-three a year earlier. Officials had feared enrollment might fall as low as twenty-five.

Among the students were two children of John Maxwell Adams, a Presbyterian minister in nearby Wallingford. The Adamses believed in public schools but thought MFS deserved support. The family later moved to Minnesota, where one of the children, Joan, married Walter Mondale, who became Jimmy Carter's vice president in 1977.

MFS records do not reveal how the school paid its bills after losing one-third of its students. It may have received quiet contributions from supporters. But the budget was not balanced again until 1943.

Little Lancess transferred to public school in September 1938. Before he left, though, the chair of the Quaker race committee replied to Sadie Alexander, defending Friends by pointing out the trouble MFS was enduring in their mutual cause.

Today, roughly one-third of the 150 students at Media–Providence Friends School are non-white.

Other Quaker schools took note. When they finally integrated—Westtown and George Schools in 1945, others later—they consulted their parents first. Some people, after all, prepare for change. Others have to *be* prepared.

1941: The Great Marcus Hook Swindle

One way or another, banks always get paid. The big banks that taxpayers bailed out during the "Great Recession" that began in 2008? According to the nonprofit Institute for Policy Studies, the twenty banks that took the most money paid their top five executives—100 individuals—an average of $13.8 million *each* from 2006 to 2008 while laying off 160,000 employees.

An anomaly? Consider the Great Marcus Hook Swindle of 1941. That was the year in which the Roosevelt administration demanded that England—defeated on the European mainland and "blitzed" by German bombers at home—give up some asset to prove to a skeptical U.S. public that it really, truly needed help. The White House itself chose Britain's largest, most profitable U.S. holding—American Viscose of Marcus Hook.

The company was quickly appraised and sold to American bankers for $54 million—a fraction of its worth. American Viscose had grossed, on average, $6.2 million annually for the previous ten years. The U.S. bankers then turned around and resold the company—whose assets alone were worth $128 million—for $62 million to American buyers. "Some Britons—most notably Winston Churchill—thought they had been fleeced," wrote business historian Ron Chernow.

The story begins with rayon, the modern term for an artificial fiber invented in 1855 by a Swiss chemist. First called "artificial silk," rayon is produced from processed wood pulp. Other inventors tinkered with the invention until, in 1894, a group of English chemists patented a process that produced a commercially viable fabric they called "viscose."

In 1941, American Viscose of Marcus Hook was the most profitable British-owned company in the United States. That made it a target when the British were told they had to earn U.S. assistance. The bankers involved cleaned up. *Ballinger Collection, Athenaeum of Philadelphia.*

Viscose was a derivation of the word viscosity, the scientific measure of a fluid's thickness. The wood pulp from which the fabric was spun was viscous, or thick. Among artificial fibers, rayon was the pioneer—far ahead of nylon (first produced in 1935), Dacron (1941), olefin (1949), polyester (1953) and others. The textile industry adopted the name rayon in 1924.

Rayon fabric was primarily used in clothing, furnishings, industry (medical products and automobile tire cord) and in personal disposables such as tampons and diapers. By the turn of the twenty-first century, its use had declined because its manufacture generates large amounts of sulfurous waste.

The British rights to Viscose were bought by Courtauld & Co., an English textile manufacturer. The market grew steadily, and in 1908, Samuel Agar Salvage (1876–1946) knocked on the door. Salvage was a thirty-two-year-old English immigrant who had come to America in 1893. He'd started out selling china and glass in Cincinnati and then moved to New York, where he worked for two different textile companies. In 1897, Salvage started his own fabric-importing business.

Among the imported fabric was some artificial silk from Germany. Salvage sold it to braid and trimming manufacturers but found no other interest. Still, he was impressed with the product. "When Samuel Courtauld & Co. started to make artificial silk, I got hold of some and sampled the trade with it," Salvage later said. He became Courtauld's U.S. sales representative in 1908. A year later, Salvage proposed that Courtauld buy the U.S. manufacturing rights for rayon and open a plant here. According to company legend, Salvage sent the proposition on a postcard.

Salvage recommended a site in Marcus Hook, probably because the Delaware River location was convenient for road, rail and ocean shipping and because costs would be less than at similar sites near New York. Previously a resort and center of shipbuilding and shad fishing, Marcus Hook had tilted toward heavy industry in the early twentieth century. By 1910, it was also home to oil refineries operated by the Sun and Union petroleum companies.

Construction of American Viscose's first factory was not yet complete when, a week before Christmas 1910, a group of Courtauld veterans sent from England got together with some raw American recruits to watch the first yarn form as the viscose solution was pumped through a spinning jet. By the next morning, the stuff was all over the floor, the walls, the benches and the ceiling.

"Only a few men who had come over from England knew how to handle the sticky, wet yarn," reported the *Times*. "Most, if not all, the rayon made on that Monday and for some time to come, went into the waste basket." But by 1916, U.S. demand had exceeded the plant's capacity. Additional plants were built in Roanoke, Virginia, Lewistown, Pennsylvania, Parkersburg, West Virginia, and Front Royal, Virginia, but Marcus Hook remained the headquarters of American Viscose.

Courtauld's patent expired in 1920, and DuPont entered the field. Competition drove down prices but expanded the market. By 1940, U.S. consumption of rayon was 488 million pounds annually, up from 61 million in 1927. And American Viscose had 31 percent of the market.

Salvage was made a Courtauld vice-president, knighted and grew rich. His 1927 mansion, Rynwood—with 127 acres, formal gardens and miles of stained glass and oak paneling—on Long Island's Gold Coast allowed him to consort with Vanderbilts. It now houses a winery.

But Marcus Hook profited, too. "The need to hire skilled, long-term workers put AVC in competition with other regional industries," according to a report by the Delaware County Planning Department, "and led to the company's decision to build a highly attractive model town where its employees could live at subsidized rents."

Winston Churchill—seen here in 1941 walking the deck of a British battleship after his Atlantic Conference with Franklin Roosevelt—thought his country had been fleeced in that year's forced sale of American Viscose of Marcus Hook. *Courtesy of Library of Congress.*

Twenty-acre American Viscose Village included 261 houses, 2 boardinghouses and a general store, designed with Flemish, Tudor and Craftsman architecture. In 1950, after the suburbanization trend had made plain Americans' new preference for homeownership, the company sold the homes to its employees. Viscose Village has been the focus of a preservation effort since the early 1990s.

Despite its success—or, perhaps, because of it—American Viscose found itself vulnerable to the combined clout of the White House and J.P. Morgan.

In the early twentieth century, J.P. Morgan was the preeminent bank in the world, a position it carefully built with its own distinctive banking practices. It catered exclusively to prominent families—Vanderbilts, DuPonts, Guggenheims, Astors—by requiring personal accounts of no less than $5 million. It had no tellers, offered no consumer loans and granted no mortgages. Usually, J.P. Morgan had no more than one office per country, although that lone outpost *was* furnished with leather armchairs, grandfather clocks and polished brass lamps.

"It never wanted to appear too eager for business," wrote Chernow. "Instead of setting up offices hither and yon, it preferred to have clients make pilgrimages to it." A Lyon businessman would travel to Paris, an English businessman to London and a Texas businessman to New York. Opening a J.P. Morgan account was like joining a club.

"The Morgan bank used to boast that 96 of America's one hundred largest corporations were clients," wrote Chernow, "and hinted that in two of the remaining cases, it had blackballed the companies as unfit."

With such clients, Morgan entwined itself in the power structure of many countries, but especially the United States, England and France. In 1895, it temporarily rigged the price of gold to keep it from falling and the country from abandoning the gold standard. In 1912, as lender to the White Star steamship company, Morgan lobbied the New York Harbor Board for a one-hundred-foot extension to a Hudson River pier so that it could receive its two new ships, *Olympic* and *Titanic*. Morgan's influence was only partially diminished by New Deal legislation that forced the company to split into a commercial banking division (J.P. Morgan) and investment banking (Morgan Stanley).

Both Morgan entities were involved when Roosevelt and his treasury secretary, Henry Morgenthau, decided that American Viscose had to go.

Following his reelection in 1940, FDR became openly committed to helping the British cause, and Lend-Lease became his formula. Rather than send money or sell arms—forbidden by the Neutrality Act—FDR proposed that the United States "lend" war materiel (ships, aircraft, tanks, munitions) in exchange for (in the case of Britain) "leases" to bases in Newfoundland, Bermuda and the West Indies.

The proposal was widely interpreted—and was—a step toward war. The country, in general, disliked Hitler but also considered Britain an imperialist power that had brought many of its problems upon itself. Both Congress and the public would require persuasion.

When Sir Frederick Phillips, a British Treasury official, visited Washington in July 1940, Morgenthau had presented him with a list of British holdings in the United States. At the top of the list—above Shell Oil, Lever Brothers, Dunlop Tire and Rubber and Brown & Williamson Tobacco—was American Viscose. Together, the companies were worth $833 million.

"How could Americans justify providing assistance to the British when the latter had such important assets in the United States?" Morgenthau asked. Phillips did not take the question seriously, but when he returned in December, the treasury secretary was more insistent. "He had to demonstrate to a still-isolationist U.S. public and Congress," wrote historian Mira Wilkins, "that

Great Britain was not asking for funds from Americans while it had its own sizable resources in this country."

The British capitulated. In London, Churchill assigned Lord Thomas S. Catto—governor of the Bank of England and (ahem!) a Morgan partner—to deliver the news. Chairman Samuel Courtauld, wrote Chernow, behaved "in exemplary fashion."

"He asked only one question: 'Was the sale essential in the national interest, whatever the hardship on him and his company?'" Catto said that it was, and Courtauld thought of England.

At J.P. Morgan's recommendation, the sale was managed by Morgan Stanley and another firm.

After the war, when Churchill described the incident in cynical terms in his memoirs, Morgan Stanley partner Harold Stanley tried to get the former prime minister to rephrase. But Churchill would not budge in his conviction that American Viscose had brought far less than it was worth.

Also after the war, and bitter litigation, Courtauld received additional compensation from the British government. Not, it should be noted, from the banks.

1942: The End of Compromise

Is there virtue in compromise? Or is that like hanging a big "Kick Me" sign on your back?

That was the question faced in 1942 by the region's African American workers. Gearing up for wartime production, Sun Ship of Chester had announced thousands of jobs for blacks building tankers and troop ships. The catch? They would work in a segregated yard.

Opting for paychecks over theory, blacks flocked to Sun. There, all-black Yard No. 4 turned out twenty transport ships in three years. But when the war was over, blacks suffered most from layoffs, according to John M. McLarnon, a historian of Delaware County politics and race relations. By late 1947, Sun Ship's wartime employment, which peaked in 1943 at thirty-five thousand workers—roughly half black—had fallen to a prewar (1939) level of only two thousand.

After the war, though, only about 25 percent of Sun workers were black— half the rate before and during the war. For their patience, blacks had actually lost ground.

Then, blacks were done with compromise. George Raymond (1914– 1999), a laid-off Yard No. 4 worker, took over Chester's NAACP and began a lifelong assault on discrimination. Of Raymond and his supporters, one journalist wrote in 1945: "They know the score far better than did their fathers and they are determined that conditions for Negroes must be better in the post-war world."

Sun Ship was founded in 1916 by Sun Oil to build tankers to carry the products of its Marcus Hook refinery. Then controlled by the Pew family,

Sun Oil bought an old shipyard at Chester and installed a relative, John G. Pew (1870–1954), as president.

The Pews were not racists. In fact, they could point to a history more enlightened than many. Family patriarch John Pew (1800–1884) was remembered in family lore as a conductor on the Underground Railroad. In the 1930s, Sun Ship employed blacks while other Chester companies hired only whites.

But Chester in the early twentieth century was one of the North's most segregated cities. Power was in the hands of an entrenched Republican machine that ruled with the support of locally born blacks who mostly accepted segregation. These blacks—considered by whites as among "the more responsible members of their race"—lived in Chester's West End and included an elite of ministers, physicians, lawyers and a few city officials.

Other blacks—born in the South, darker skinned, less educated and less respectful—lived in "Bethel Court," Chester's red-light district. Filled with dilapidated tenements, Bethel Court was the place to gamble, drink, buy and use drugs or find a prostitute. (The opening in 2006 of a casino at the site of Sun Ship continues at least part of this Chester tradition.) It was a dangerous place, but the housing was cheap.

Growth attracted many new residents. Baldwin Locomotive, Chester and Sun shipyards, Sun Oil, Westinghouse and Scott Paper all caused the population jump from about thirty-eight thousand in 1910 to fifty-eight thousand in 1920. Chester's black population grew from fewer than five thousand to a high of twenty thousand during the World War I boom before falling to just over seven thousand in 1920. Most new black residents ended up in Bethel Court.

As a teen, Raymond shined shoes in "the Court," witnessing beatings, murders, Klan parades and police corruption. He attended segregated grade schools and graduated from integrated Chester High in 1933 and then studied business administration at Drexel Institute until forced to drop out during the Depression. Raymond did odd jobs until going to work for the Chester Boys Club. He also joined the sedate local NAACP.

In June 1941—just as the World War II military buildup was beginning—Franklin Roosevelt issued an executive order prohibiting racial discrimination by military contractors. By May 1942, Sun was hiring sixty blacks per week and working toward a goal of six thousand black employees.

Then, another announcement: "Sun Shipbuilding corporation announced construction of a new shipyard which will be staffed by…Negro workers," reported the *New York Times*. "John G. Pew said that at first the laborers

Despite protests, most African American workers decided that a job in Sun Ship's segregated Yard No. 4 was better than no job. Here, some Yard No. 4 workers listen to a supervisor in 1943. *Courtesy of Sun Ship Historical Society.*

will be under the supervision of white personnel but Negro help on the company's payroll will be trained for promotion to these supervisory posts."

An all-black yard. Sun Ship already had three separate yards along the Delaware. Blacks worked in them all, mostly in unskilled and menial positions. Now, the shipyard needed more capacity, and John G. Pew, its president, had determined to concentrate most of Sun's black workers in the new facility, Yard No. 4.

Though progressive for the time, Pew was nevertheless a conservative man. Like other conservatives, he disliked talk about equality with its potential for social disruption. Instead, he supported the disciples of Tuskegee Institute founder Booker T. Washington (1856–1915), who had believed work was the only solution to racial prejudice.

In the 1895 address in Atlanta known as his "Compromise Speech," Washington told a mostly white audience that "the opportunity to earn a dollar in a factory just now is worth infinitely more than the opportunity to spend a dollar in an opera-house."

Opposing this theory were more radical black leaders such as W.E.B. DuBois, who said Washington "tended to shift the burden of the Negro problem to the Negro's shoulders" rather than to white racism, where it belonged.

Tellingly, Pew hired Washington's former secretary, Emmett J. Scott (1873–1957), to oversee recruitment and hiring for Yard No. 4. During World War I, Scott had served as a "confidential advisor" on Negro affairs in the War Department, where he advocated—to the extent possible—for

OCTOBER 1943

Our Yard

SUN SHIPBUILDING & DRY DOCK COMPANY · CHESTER, PA.

Sun Ship boasted of its all-black Yard No. 4 in a 1943 company newspaper—illustrated by Yard No. 4 employee William Smith—but laid off a disproportionate share of African American workers after the war. *Courtesy of Sun Ship Historical Society.*

black soldiers. His subsequent book, *The American Negro in World War I*, related how Scott helped avert violence near a southern military base after a black infantryman was beaten for entering a white hotel to buy a newspaper. Solution: rather than affirm its right to train U.S. soldiers at a U.S. military base on U.S. soil, the army shipped the partially trained regiment to Europe.

Secretary of War Newton Baker's foreword to Scott's book advised African American veterans that "if there have been some things which you think were not as they should have been, you must try to forget them and go back to civil life with the determination to do your part to make the country what it should be."

Philosophy aside, there was a wartime imperative to keep up production. Attempts at integration had caused race riots during World War I. When the Philadelphia Transportation Co. hired eight black motormen in 1942, a wildcat strike by six thousand white employees paralyzed the system. Pushing integration too far might simply mean that Sun didn't get any ships built.

Most black leaders were not persuaded. The black *Chicago Defender* newspaper opposed Yard No. 4 because it positioned blacks as an "auxiliary race," threatened their position in the labor movement and encouraged southern segregation. "Are these jobs worth the selling of the principles?" asked John Ross, president of the North Philadelphia Civic Association. New York congressman Adam Clayton Powell said blacks "viewed with resentment the creation of Yard No. 4."

The NAACP split on the issue. The national office condemned "Jim-Crow Shipbuilders," but Herman Laws, president of its Chester chapter, publicly supported Yard No. 4. "We feel that this is the first step toward the desired end of total integration on a non-racial basis," wrote Laws, who was later ordered to retract his support.

Even the CIO union protested, claiming that Pew's plan violated Roosevelt's order. But this went nowhere. Segregation in workplace assignments was not illegal, only discrimination in hiring.

In May 1943, Sun heralded Yard No. 4's first ship, *Marine Eagle*, as the "first ocean-going vessel in the long history of American shipbuilding to be all-Negro constructed." The last ship, *Marine Runner*, was launched in May 1945, after which Sun began the long series of layoffs in which Pew had promised race would not be a factor.

A postwar report by Scott's office declared Yard No. 4 a success. New skills were learned. Good wages were earned. Prejudice crumbled. And any problems were at least half the responsibility of blacks who, claimed the report, "often had a chip on their shoulders." But a Maritime Commission report noted hostility between workers and supervisors. As it turned out, no blacks had been advanced to management, despite early promises.

And Yard No. 4 turnout was low. During its thirty-three-month life, the yard's eight ways produced just 20 ships—an average of 2.5 ships per way. In the same period, Sun's other three yards produced 132 ships, or 6.6 vessels on each of its twenty ways. Part of the reason was that Yard No. 4 built complicated C-4 transports—destined to transport tanks or troops or serve as hospital ships—while other yards built simpler tankers. But the Maritime Commission concluded that Yard No. 4's low productivity was mostly due to racially tinged labor strife and poor worker-management relations.

Raymond took over the Chester NAACP in 1942 and broke its ties to the Republican machine. In 1945, he launched efforts to desegregate public services by leading groups of well-dressed blacks into Chester's restaurants and movie theaters, where they answered demands that they move by referring to the state's seldom-enforced civil rights laws. Later drives opened up the city's public housing and schools.

In 1958, Raymond bought a house in Rutledge that burned the day before he was to move in. The borough then tried to claim the site by eminent domain for a new town hall. But Raymond, a veteran of Yard No. 4, fought off the effort, rebuilt the house and moved in the next year.

Compromise, he knew, gets you nowhere.

1955: What Kids Want

What do kids like? Corporations spend millions to find out. But William John Clifton Haley Jr. (1925–1981) just listened. Then he used what he had learned to invent rock-and-roll.

In 1952, packing up after a gig at Eddystone High School, the leader of a little-known "rockabilly" band asked a member of the audience what he thought of the performance. It was, the kid answered, "like crazy, man, crazy." Crazy meant very good, the fifties equivalent of "awesome."

Haley wrote down the phrase. Then the young musician from Booth's Corner drove home and, with a fellow band member, began throwing tunes and lyrics together. Written in thirty minutes, "Crazy Man, Crazy" was recorded in April 1953. It was the first rock-and-roll recording to appear on U.S. musical charts, peaking at number twelve.

But the blockbuster came two years later when Haley and his band—the Comets—released "Rock Around the Clock," the biggest-selling rock-and-roll single of all time. At least twenty-five million were sold, according to the *Guinness Book of World Records*. Among all vinyl records, that would place "Rock Around the Clock" second only to Bing Crosby's 1942 "White Christmas." An estimated one hundred million copies were sold in other forms. Supposedly, "Rock Around the Clock" is playing somewhere in the world every minute of the day.

Born near Detroit, Haley was the son of an auto mechanic from Kentucky who played country music on mandolin and banjo. His mother had studied classical piano in her native England and played the church organ. In 1929, after the elder Haley lost his job, the family moved to Boothwyn to stay with

Bill Haley (front) of Booth's Corner spent his early career with cowboy bands like the Four Western Aces. But an agent looking for cross-cultural appeal suggested a Space Age allusion to Halley's Comet, and the band became "Bill Haley and the Comets." *Courtesy of Bill Haley Museum, Munich, Germany.*

relatives. Haley Sr. eventually found a twenty-five-cent-per-hour factory job and moved his family to Chester and, in 1933, to Booth's Corner.

Haley was a loner. When he was four, a bungled ear operation severed an optic nerve, leaving him blind in the left eye. No one noticed until one day when Haley was looking up at a passing airplane, his father noticed he was shading only one eye.

His was a Tom Sawyer sort of childhood. Haley swam in Naaman's Creek and played in the woods, but his partial blindness made him unsuited for sports. He couldn't hit or catch a baseball. Instead, he preferred to read adventure books and dream of becoming famous. His parents gave him a guitar, which he played when the family sang together and carried everywhere.

Once, a group of local girls chanced upon Haley giving a "concert" in the woods. "After Billy sang each song, he would bow as if pretending the trees were his audience," one told biographer John von Hoelle. "Then, one of the girls coughed or something and Billy, who didn't know we were there, looked startled and ran home."

Given Haley's background, his success in show business is remarkable. In 1940, he quit school after the eighth grade to work at a bottling plant, filling five-gallon bottles for thirty-five cents an hour. Later, Haley drove a delivery truck. "The day Bill Haley got his driver's license, the people of Booth's Corner began walking on the telephone lines," said former co-worker Bob Miles. "Boy, did Bill like to drive fast."

Haley's first stage performance, in 1941, was at an amateur night sponsored by Siloam Methodist Church. It was a disaster. Haley had fallen on his bicycle and damaged his guitar. Only four strings worked. He lost to a teen who played "Wreck of the Old 97" on harmonica. Haley didn't play in public again for two years, and then by accident.

In 1943, Haley was doing odd jobs around the Booth's Corner farmers market. The owner had heard that the eighteen-year-old had a good voice and requested a private performance. Unbeknownst to Haley, the man had switched on his microphone to the market sound system. When the locals heard "Has Anyone Seen My Gal?" and "My Old Kentucky Home" pouring from the speakers, many thought Gene Autry was on the radio.

Soon, Haley was dressed like his singing cowboy heroes, standing on a wooden table in the parking lot and singing for five dollars an hour. It was a gimmick to attract market traffic, but it made Haley a star in the neighborhood.

The following ten years were lean. After his day job—now at Baldwin Locomotive—Haley sang at birthday parties and picnics. Gradually, his gigs became more impressive. He opened a concert for Roy Rogers and the Sons of the Pioneers before a crowd of ten thousand. He learned to yodel and traveled with a series of cowboy bands—the Texas Range Riders, Cousin Lee's Band, the Down Homers and the Range Drifters.

But singing in bars was a hard life. Haley drank too much and had a string of one-night girlfriends. But he also learned about music: jazz-hillbilly in the Oklahoma oil fields, rhythm-and-blues in East St. Louis, Latin-flavored Tex-Mex in South Texas, Dixieland in New Orleans. Somewhere on the road, his band dissolved. In 1946, Haley arrived home in Booth's Corner, sick, broke and discouraged.

"I wasn't getting anywhere," he later recalled. "I needed to get a steady job, forget my foolish ideas and accomplish something that was real." For thirty dollars a week, he took the first of several jobs as a radio disc jockey. The first jobs were short because station owners objected to Haley's music choices, especially the sounds one dismissed as "jig-a-boo" music. His break came in 1947 when a new station, WPWA, opened in Chester, with an owner who wanted to reach the factory town's ethnically mixed workers. Haley became musical director, which included selling ads, maintaining a record library, hiring DJs and sweeping up.

With a steady, though grueling, job to sustain him, Haley resumed live performances. New groups—the Four Aces of Western Swing and then the Saddlemen—experimented with sounds Haley had heard on the road. Traditional country music audiences disliked these innovations, but bar crowds were different. Beginning in 1950, the Saddlemen began an eighteen-month run at Gloucester City's Twin Bar, where the volume, instrumental technique and driving beat of what Haley called "cowboy jive" drew a new following.

At the Twin, they played "Rock the Joint," an old song retooled with lyrics about knocking down walls, getting high and jitterbugging "until the law come knocking." The Saddlemen replaced its original shuffle with a rrroom-pah beat and leaned heavy on the bass.

"It was our private joke," Haley later said. "Then I looked around and, so help me, people were dancing. I turned to the guys and asked, 'What on earth did I do?'"

Not everyone liked it. "It was a shame how they abused their instruments," said one woman. "I was a music teacher, and no real musicians treat their instruments like that."

But Dave Miller did like it. The president of Palda Records had been looking for white men who could play like black men. He offered a recording contract but insisted they ramp up the sound still more and ditch the cowboy image.

"With a name like yours, you ought to call yourselves the Comets," Miller told Haley, noting the similarity of his name and that of Halley's Comet. The Space Age was dawning. Interest in the heavens crossed cultural lines that cowboy music did not.

"Rock Around the Clock" was not a new song, or even the first of the name. According to historian Jim Dawson, the song was heir to rhythms and lyrics long popular in jazz circles, where the word "rock" was a synonym for sexual intercourse. In 1922, black vaudevillian Trixie Smith recorded "My Man Rocks Me," which included lines like this:

My daddy rocks me in a steady jelly roll
My daddy rocks me and he never lets go
I look at the clock and the clock strikes eight
Oh, daddy, take it out before it gets too late.

By the 1950s, "rock" was a musical buzzword for producers and musicians looking for acceptable ways to bring black music to white audiences. The product had to be cleansed of sexual references but maintain its danceable beat. As a form of test marketing, the Comets played free at high schools. "I knew I was on the right track because the kids began clapping in rhythm and yelling 'Go! Go! Go!' as they dug that beat," Haley told the *Philadelphia Bulletin* in 1953.

Written in 1952, the song recorded by the Comets had sunk quickly when recorded conventionally by another performer. Haley thought his group could do better. But Miller refused to record "Rock Around the Clock" because he had previously had contract disputes with its co-author. The Comets eventually left Miller.

"Rock Around the Clock" was recorded in Manhattan at a 1954 session that was nearly cancelled when the band was two hours late. The Chester-Bridgeport Ferry carrying them across the Delaware got stuck on a sandbar. (The Commodore Barry Bridge was not yet built.) Another group was waiting for the studio, so the Comets recorded two quick versions. Neither was perfect, but technicians mixed them. Then the song was released as the B side, which most DJs ignored. And the record company labeled it a fox trot!

The adults screwed up. But teens saved "Rock Around the Clock." In 1955, director Richard Brooks made it the soundtrack for his teen-rebellion movie *Blackboard Jungle*. "Rock Around the Clock" soon became wildly popular around the world. In Liverpool, fourteen-year-old John Lennon first heard it on the radio while lying on his bed. "It just grabbed me, like mentally," the former Beatle remembered in an interview published in 1981. "That afternoon I borrowed a few bob and bought the record. That was when I knew I wanted to go into pop music."

For that, and much that followed, the 1950s teenagers of the Delaware Valley—your parents or grandparents, perhaps—deserve a share of the world's thanks.

1964: Hey, Hey, LBJ

Politics is a series of temporary alliances. And few alliances have been more temporary than that of Lyndon Johnson (1908–1973) and the Swarthmore College community. Don't be fooled by the enthusiasm of the people with the signs in that photo. They were probably all townies. When Johnson arrived to address the college's centennial commencement in 1964, many who listened were actually in despair.

"Liberalism is the way of the future," lamented Peter Passell, a Swarthmore junior, journalist and self-described radical who, that autumn, compromised himself by distributing Republicans for Johnson literature at area Goldwater rallies. Yes, Passell assured readers of the *Phoenix* student newspaper, he would have preferred a far more radical choice. But "which is more likely to win over a reluctant Congress?" Passell asked. "The soothing platitudes of Lyndon Johnson pleading for a Great Society, or…a thousand pickets in Washington?"

And that was the height of Johnson's popularity. Four years later, he no longer made college appearances.

Johnson was filling in for John F. Kennedy, who had been invited before his assassination. But LBJ had his own goal: selling the "War on Poverty" announced at his January State of the Union address. In August, Congress would pass legislation creating Head Start, food stamps, work study, Medicare and Medicaid, at a cost then forecast at $1 billion a year. The *Phoenix* later fretted that the only result might be to "settle a federal bureaucracy onto the poor."

In his fifteen-minute speech, Johnson tied his plans to the historical good deeds of the Quakers who had founded Swarthmore and then attacked

Despite the apparent enthusiasm when Lyndon Johnson appeared at Swarthmore's 1964 commencement, LBJ was never popular at the college. And opinions of his presidency would drop still further. *Courtesy of Swarthmore College.*

the idea that poverty was beyond federal authority. "Does government subvert our freedom through the Social Security system which guards our people against destitution when they are too old to work? Does government undermine our freedom by bringing electricity to the farm, by controlling floods or by ending bank failures?" Johnson asked. "The truth is, far from crushing the individual, government at its best liberates him from the enslaving forces of his environment."

Then he was gone. As the crowd applauded, Johnson rode a waiting limo down the hill to his helicopter, waiting on the soccer field.

LBJ has been quoted as having said, "An honest politician is one who, when he's bought, stays bought." This statement actually came from Simon Cameron, Lincoln's secretary of war. But it *could* have been Johnson, whose skill at political arm-twisting made him an effective Senate majority leader. "The greatest intelligence gatherer Washington has ever known," according to historian Randall Woods, Johnson knew where every senator stood, his philosophy and prejudices, his strengths and weaknesses and what it took to break him. And he loved to give electric toothbrushes to friends. "For then I know," Johnson explained, "that from now until the end of their days, they will think of me the first thing in the morning and the last at night."

Few politicians crossed Lyndon Johnson.

But such tactics didn't work with Swarthmoreans, whose institution pledged them only to what it still describes as the "search of truth." Not the actual truth, of course. That is endlessly debatable. Swarthmore's idea is that the individual should constantly reconsider, apply and test what he or she believes. It's not a mission that is likely to breed much respect for dogma or authority.

Indeed, Swarthmore students have always crossed their professors and administrators and been praised for doing so. One example, related in the *Phoenix* in 1964, occurred during the 1921–40 presidency of Frank Aydelotte (1880–1956). A campus club had invited an African American minister to speak and asked Aydelotte to join the group for dinner. Cross-racial socializing was unusual, so Aydelotte, concerned that the minister might be treated rudely by someone, proposed that the man dine at his house instead.

Word of Aydelotte's proposal resulted in an outraged *Phoenix* editorial: "It is the timorous attitude that tolerance can best be served by shielding intolerance to which we take exception," argued the paper. "That is the easy downhill path of expediency; it ruffles no tempers, causes no enmity, disturbs no one's tranquility. Neither does it serve the cause of race tolerance."

The next day, Aydelotte summoned the editor to his office—and apologized. The editorial was absolutely right, the fiftyish educator told the twenty-something undergrad, and he hereby withdrew his offer. And, by the way, did the young man think the matter required a public apology? The student editor assured Aydelotte that word would get around on its own.

In 1964, the voting age was twenty-one years, so the only ballots most Swarthmore students could cast that fall were in a campus mock election. Johnson won 94 percent of the vote, dwarfing his 61 percent share in the general election. But enthusiasm? Not much. On campus, Johnson's top qualification was that he was not Goldwater, who represented a phenomenon Swarthmore didn't understand.

Passell was perplexed by the venom he encountered leafleting for Johnson at a Republican rally, where people hissed "communist" and told him he had no right to be there. Professor George E. Von der Muhll called Goldwater's nomination "an act of recklessness so unprecedented as to raise doubts about the GOP's intention of seriously contesting future elections." The *Phoenix* observed, "We are not so much afraid of [Goldwater] and his closeness to the presidency, as of the forces which have made his ascendancy possible."

But the election was not students' top concern. Indeed, on election day, members of the college's Students for a Democratic Society (SDS) chapter were buttonholing voters for a "voluntary poll tax" to fund voter registration drives in the South the following summer. According to the *Phoenix*, they collected $352. Two Swarthmore students—Ellen Arguimbau '66 and Gretchen Schwarz '65—later returned from drives in Humphreys County, Mississippi, with tales of fleeing from pickups full of angry rednecks.

Closer to hand was the segregated city of Chester. In the summer of 1963, Stanley Branche (1933–1992), a local black activist, and members of the Swarthmore SDS traveled to Maryland to attend workshops on community organizing. They came back and organized blockades that shut down Chester's dilapidated (and all-black) Franklin School. Most protesters were black, but Swarthmore students were usually in the ranks. "I remember spending several days in jail with my school books from Swarthmore, attempting to do my homework and study," Miriam Feingold Real '63 told the *Phoenix* in 2009.

Things intensified as the Vietnam War escalated. During this period, campus news seemed increasingly squeezed out of the *Phoenix* as the paper bannered stories such as "Student arrested by FBI for refusal to register"— even if the student in question was in California.

In April 1965, 180 Swarthmore students were among 20,000 protesting the war at a Washington rally MC'd by Paul Booth, a 1964 graduate. Counter-protesters from the American Nazi Party greeted them with signs reading "Peace Creeps Go Home."

College supervision of students' personal lives was a long-standing issue in the sixties. Female students were then required to be in their dorms after 10 p.m., and men were not permitted in women's rooms. And when, on special occasions, the genders did mix, residence officials were expected to confirm that three of every four feet were on the floor and every door open the width of a book. "Some students tried to use a 'book' of matches," recalled Chris Densmore, later curator of Swarthmore's Friends Historical Library.

Historically, Quakers had been conservative about personal morality, so college trustees worried that relaxing these rules would damage the school's image. Increasingly, though, Swarthmore students simply refused to obey, arguing— as one *Phoenix* editorial put it—that "under the present system, Swarthmore women do not have the full opportunity to form their own moral code."

In 1965, when two students were caught with beer and in mixed company after hours, several members of the student disciplinary committee to which their case was referred refused to participate in their punishment.

Eventually, of course, the college surrendered. Today, the college has "gender-neutral" restrooms in which men and women may use adjacent stalls. Incoming freshmen learn that "sexiling"—locking out a roommate to be alone with a lover—is bad manners. And contraceptives are available at the health center.

But always there was the war and a seemingly endless cycle of action and reaction.

In December 1965, state senator Clarence D. Bell of Delaware County publicly urged the Selective Service System to withdraw draft deferments from Swarthmore students who led antiwar protests. Their "bad judgment," said Bell, meant they could not be good future leaders.

In 1967, Swarthmore junior John Braxton helped enrage conservatives by joining a Quaker group that sailed a private yacht from Hong Kong to North Vietnam with medical supplies. Back home, Braxton told of visiting a residential area hit by U.S. bombing. "We saw about six blocks which were completely destroyed, killing more than a dozen," Braxton told the *Phoenix*. "I felt ashamed to be an American who was not putting all of his efforts into stopping the war."

In February 1968, forty students turned out to cheer Swarthmorean Vin Berg as he took a pre-draft physical. Berg had renounced his student deferment because it discriminated against those who couldn't afford college and planned to refuse induction. In March, William Sloane Coffin could, without much fear of contradiction, open his Swarthmore address saying, "I'll assume that all of you believe that the war in Vietnam is militarily a mess and morally a catastrophe." Coffin, a former Yale chaplain who had run the first Peace Corps training programs and organized southern Freedom Rides, had recently been indicted for counseling draft evasion.

In the fall of 1968, returning Swarthmore students shared street experiences from August's Democratic National Convention in Chicago. Howard Gold told the *Phoenix* of being barred from the Conrad Hilton hotel by a policeman as he sought water after being gassed. "I was furious," said Gold. "'Pig!' I screamed. It was the first time I had used the word all week."

The college didn't even bother with a mock election that year.

1973: The Odd Couple

Odd pairings are legendary. There's Bill and Hillary. Jimmy Carter and his beer-drinking brother, Billy. And then there is Andrew Wyeth (1917–2009) and his brother, Nat. One was an artist famed for his depictions of the parched winter landscapes of Maine and Chadds Ford. The other is responsible for much of the litter that mars those landscapes.

Nathaniel Wyeth (1912–1990), an engineer who spent his career with DuPont, invented the plastic soda bottle. That is the bottle—patented in 1973—whose manufacture, according to the Container Recycling Institute, requires 1.5 million barrels of oil annually, has only a one-in-five chance of being recycled and—because its contents are usually consumed on the go—is frequently littered.

During his career, Wyeth invented or was the co-inventor of twenty-five products and processes in plastics, textile fibers, electronics and mechanical systems. Among his honors was the 1981 outstanding achievement award from the Society of Plastics Engineers for invention of the PET (polyethylene-terephthalate) bottle. In 1986, he was elected to the Plastics Hall of Fame. He was a Fellow of the American Society of Mechanical Engineers.

"Very seldom do [ideas] come out of nowhere," Wyeth told interviewer Kenneth A. Brown in the 1980s. "It's usually a culmination of one thought after another that leads to a solution and a complete understanding of the problem."

Well, perhaps not 100 percent "complete."

The third child of Carolyn and Newell Convers (N.C.) Wyeth, Nathaniel Wyeth was initially named for his father. But the boy's parents went to court before he reached age five and had his name legally changed.

A plastic beverage bottle—invented by Andrew Wyeth's brother, Nathaniel—litters the driveway at Kuerner Farm, frequently painted by the artist. *Courtesy of Mark E. Dixon.*

The Wyeths' first clue that their child was different was the baby's dirty hands. It was the Wyeths' habit to put toddler Nat out on a sunny, enclosed porch in a baby carriage for his daily nap. But his hands were always greasy when they got him up. "One day…they kept an eye on me," Wyeth said later. "Then, they noticed me lean over the side of the coach, reach down and move the wheels with my hands." By turning the wheels, the little boy made the coach move from one end of the porch to the other. Back and forth, over and over, and dirtying his hands in the process.

"I don't know why we should encumber this boy with an artist's name when he's undoubtedly going to be an engineer," said his father. "Look at his understanding of those wheels and the way he's moving that coach!" So, Newell Convers Wyeth Jr. became Nathaniel Convers Wyeth—a name he shared with a paternal uncle who was an engineer.

Throughout his life, Wyeth dismissed the notion—posed repeatedly—that his father might have been disappointed that he didn't paint. "The only thing he insisted on was that whatever we did, we should do it with all our hearts, with all our might," he said.

And he did. As a boy, Wyeth cannibalized "I don't know how many" alarm clocks for parts to build model speedboats. He used an airplane propeller to drive a pontoon boat. And he built a "sea sled"—six feet long with a curved bow and an outboard motor—so fast the Wyeths dubbed it "Ex-Lax." When the Wyeths sailed to Monhegan Island during their Maine summers, Nat went along in Ex-Lax, doing circles around the family's larger, slower powerboat. "The local paper," said Wyeth, "wrote that I had taken Ex-Lax and gone to Monhegan," a description that confused or offended some readers. "It sounded terrible."

Later, Nat expanded on the curved-bow idea to build a twenty-foot hydroplane. N.C. Wyeth provided a Ford V-8 engine, and when the craft was launched, the artist personally waded into the frigid Maine waters to christen his son's *Silver Foil* with champagne. "He was so excited that he forgot to take his watch out," said Wyeth, "and it just got soaked."

Silver Foil reached forty-five to fifty miles per hour but never had quite enough power to plane—that is, to lift out of the water. "It had a manual transmission, and we just couldn't shift it fast enough," said Wyeth. (Lesson learned.)

Wyeth earned bachelor's and master's degrees in mechanical engineering from Penn, a school recommended by another engineer uncle, Stimson Wyeth. After college, he joined Delco, a Dayton, Ohio auto parts company recommended by his namesake Uncle Nathaniel.

At Delco, Wyeth made a good impression early on by solving a production problem in the manufacture of Sani-Flush, the toilet bowl cleaner. One of the ingredients kept plugging a valve in a machine that mixed the cleaner. The valve—essentially a gate or door—crossed from one side of a pipe to the other but sometimes couldn't close entirely because the gritty, acidic material was in the way.

Wyeth replaced the single-gate valve with a two-door version. The two doors met in the middle of the pipe where the material was moving fastest and less likely to clog. That got Wyeth a promotion to Delco's R&D lab to work on new concepts and devices. It was exactly where he wanted to be—but at DuPont, near his home, not in Ohio. So, in 1936, as soon as an opportunity arose, Wyeth jumped ship.

At DuPont, Wyeth's first invention was a machine that filled cardboard tubes with gunpowder to make dynamite. Previously, the process involved a lot of manual labor, requiring that employees be exposed to nitroglycerine, which dilates blood vessels (its medical purpose) and creates painful headaches. DuPont wanted to minimize this exposure.

Wyeth built a prototype that impressed his boss, who, in turn, showed it to the explosives supervisor. The higher-ups then authorized construction of a final version. "That was music to my ears," said Wyeth. "When they left, I did a dance right there in the room, jumping up and down. To see an idea finally go into motion is one of the most gratifying experiences I think anyone can have."

The plastic soda bottle was purely Wyeth's idea. Informed that plastic couldn't withstand the pressure of carbonation, Wyeth wanted to see for himself. He went home, filled an empty detergent bottle with ginger ale and put it in the refrigerator overnight. The next morning, the bottle was so swollen that it had become trapped. Wyeth couldn't remove it until he had carefully bled off some of the built-up pressure. "No wonder they don't put carbonated beverages in plastic bottles," he realized. "They're too weak."

Wyeth knew that plastic could be strong. Previously, he'd been involved in the development of Typar, a polypropylene sheeting material used as backing for rugs, for building wrap, to cover muddy areas before pouring concrete and as landscape fabric to suppress weeds. (In the rug industry, Typar destroyed the market for imported jute.) Typar is made in wide rolls, and Wyeth's contribution was to develop a way to prevent deflection (bending) in the rollers that squeezed the plastic fibers together. His solution: magnets. Wyeth gave one roller a southern polarity and the other a northern one. That drew the rollers together naturally, eliminated deflection and allowed operators to increase or decrease pressure merely by adjusting the power to the magnets.

"I think we got four or five good, solid patents on that," he said. "It was sort of like child's play when you think that this idea's been around for years and nobody used it."

From his experience working with nylon, Wyeth knew that the strength of plastic increases when it is stretched. When making nylon thread, for instance, stretching causes the molecules in the material to line up. But unlike thread, which needs to be strong in only one direction, plastic bottles need to be strong biaxially—that is, from top to bottom and from side to side.

Wyeth solved the problem with what he called a "preform" mold, which looked like a test tube with screw threads on the inside. Rather than running in a single spiral, however, the mold had two sets that crossed each other in a diamond crisscross pattern. When the plastic was extruded through this mold, its molecules aligned in the biaxial fashion that Wyeth intended.

"It took a lot of experimentation," he said. Working with one assistant and a handpress, Wyeth produced many shapeless globs of plastic and, later, some truly ugly containers. "I remember bringing some of those samples over to my boss," recalled Wyeth. "He'd ask, 'Is this all you've done for $50,000?'" Wyeth later estimated that he had made ten thousand attempts.

Success came late in the day. The lab was dimly lit. Wyeth and his assistant opened the mold, expecting more shapeless globs of resin. Instead, the mold seemed to be empty. They looked closer and found a crystal clear bottle. "Since then, I have seen countless truly beautiful PET bottles," said Wyeth. "But none of them will ever be as memorable as the first."

That first bottle was polypropylene, which, as his final improvement, Wyeth replaced with PET. PET has superior elastic properties but is permeable to carbon dioxide over time. Put a Coke on the shelf for six months and it will go flat. That never happened when soda was bottled in glass. It's why soft drinks now have expiration dates.

By 1980, production of plastic beverage bottles had exploded to 2.5 billion containers; by 1985, to 5.5 billion units. Glass became obsolete. Plastics experts predict that the PET bottle will eventually be standard for wine, liquor, beer and many other products. And, of course, for roadsides.

1975: A DIFFERENT SORT OF SERVICE

War demands different sorts of service. Some people create orphans; others care for them. Generally, the second crowd seems to enjoy its work more.

Years later, Grace Kight recalled the 1975 collapse of South Vietnam as a high point in her life. It was that May that she and a platoon of volunteers—many of them former war protesters—met a bus filled with war orphans that had rolled into Media and stopped at her house.

Kight had every reason to send the bus elsewhere. She was the middle-aged mother of five teenaged children with a husband recovering from a heart attack. But four of the Kight children had been adopted from Korea, the abandoned mixed-race children of U.S. soldiers. Kight knew what the kids from Saigon were coming from and what they were facing.

"My husband said, 'Grace, if you think you can cope with this, go ahead,'" said Kight. "So, I got back on the phone to say, 'No, I couldn't possibly,' and instead said, 'Sure.'" A Quaker, Kight feels she got a divine nudge. "It was the same sort of nudge I got for each of our kids," she said. "It was just a bigger nudge."

When Stan and Grace Kight took in their first orphan, they were fortyish Drexel University professors with one biological daughter, Kristin, born in 1958. They wanted another child, but domestic adoption agencies said they were too old. In 1961, they had discovered Welcome House, the Bucks County agency founded in 1949 by writer Pearl S. Buck to find homes for Asian orphans. Two years later, they took home two-and-a-half-year-old Tony, who had blonde hair and a Korean face. "We started with

When college professor Grace Kight (center, with child) told her students that she would be caring for seventy mixed-race children whisked out of a collapsing South Vietnam in April 1975, more than fifty volunteered to help. *Courtesy of Monica Gosling.*

the idea of adopting one child," said Kight, "and ended up adopting four within two years."

Abandoned as an infant at a Seoul orphanage, Tony's biracial looks made his adoption in Korea unlikely. At age three, he was scheduled to move to an institution for older children. "Everyone—including the U.S. Army chaplains and the Korean police—told us that would have gotten him killed," recalled Kight. "The orphanage was crammed with [older] kids who killed children who looked American."

A year later, the Kights attended one of Welcome House's annual reunions at Buck's Green Hills Farm. There were exhibits and workshops going on in the barn, and the couple agreed that Stan would check them out while Grace stayed outside with Tony. Stan soon reappeared. "You have to see this," he said.

In the barn was a bulletin board covered with photos of Korean orphans. A sign read: "These children are in desperate need. Can you help?" Down in a lower corner was a picture of a little girl with light brown Caucasian hair and the saddest face that Grace had ever seen.

"When I went outside and joined my husband, he looked at me and said, 'You found her, didn't you?'" she recalled. "We'd both fallen in love with her picture. She was just so woebegone."

The Kights called the next morning and learned that Amy, five, had a brother, Tom, twelve, whose photo had fallen off the bulletin board. Few adoptive parents want a child that old, but the agency didn't want to separate the two.

They paused.

Finally, Stan spoke: "The only thing wrong with that little girl is that she has a brother and the only thing wrong with him is that he's twelve," he told Grace. "And those are rotten reasons to be condemned to a hopeless life." The Kights took both children.

Having now adopted three children, the Kights had passed all bureaucratic hurdles. Unbeknownst to them, that put them at the top of the agency's list of people to call in desperate cases. In 1965, the phone rang: there was an abandoned baby boy in a North Jersey hospital. Would they take him?

"He'd been born to an unmarried fifteen-year-old mother whose parents told her she was welcome to come home after giving birth, but not with the baby," explained Kight. "He didn't get any bonding at all and was being handled by twenty-four people a day. The doctors felt he was dying."

They named him Nicholas.

"He was skin and bones, no fat padding at all," recalled Kight. "He was covered with eczema, hadn't been heard to cry for days and had been steadily losing weight since birth." Kight fed him diluted goat's milk every thirty minutes with a medicine dropper. By the following Tuesday, he had gained several ounces.

"And he's the one who visits me once a week without fail," she said.

Nicholas married a Japanese woman and, in 2005, lived in Media. Tony, a building contractor, also lived in Media with his wife and adopted son. Amy, married with a son, lived in Chicago and worked in mental health research. Kristin, married with two daughters, worked with learning-disabled children and lived in Baltimore. Tom died in an auto wreck at age nineteen. Stan Kight died in 1996.

The Kights opposed the Vietnam War. Virtually everyone they knew did. They belonged to Concord Friends Meeting, whose members had been among the first to organize protests in West Chester, where they read the names of dead U.S. soldiers from the courthouse steps.

Once, in the mid-sixties, the president of the county commission teamed with the Pagans motorcycle gang to intimidate the demonstrators: one cut off power to their loudspeaker while the others revved their motorcycles to drown out their voices. The protesters continued *a capella* and, according to local historian (and Concord member) Hi Doty, attracted sympathizers "who soon were muttering their own mutters of support, and returning taunt for taunt with the bikers across the street."

With jobs and five children, the Kights had no time for such things. Instead, they helped sabotage the war effort by sheltering draft dodgers at their summer home on Nantucket. In the late sixties, young men whose draft numbers had been called often used the island to lay low before going to Canada. "There were several dozen living in the forests on the island," she recalled. "Unfortunately, many of them came thinking of warm beaches, and it gets cold at night on Nantucket." Local Quakers provided food and blankets and found some of them odd jobs. The Kights hired several to design and build a guest cottage.

Back home, the Kights moved from rural Concordville—where there weren't enough people to form a carpool—to a seventeen-room house in Media, where the kids took the trolley to school. It had four full baths, which would prove useful.

On a Friday evening in April 1975, they got another phone call. It was the agency's executive director. "She said there was a plane in the air with seventy children and that Welcome House had no place to put them when they arrived," said Kight. "Could I help?"

South Vietnam was falling. Officials who had long frustrated U.S. adoption efforts were fleeing. Freed of their oversight, Washington

Volunteers who cared for seventy South Vietnamese orphans in April 1975—including Monica Gosling, center—all thanked organizer Grace Kight afterward for letting them "take part in this terrific thing." *Courtesy of Monica Gosling.*

organized Operation Babylift to evacuate thousands of Amerasian children. Meanwhile, orphanages were swelling with additional children as refugees fled south from the northern provinces.

Cherie Clark, a Babylift nurse, described the evacuation: "We could not pull the buses near enough to the plane because there were constant, incoming rockets," wrote Clark, who described waiting for hours in one-hundred-degree heat while babies died around her.

Finally, "we were loaded onto a [C-130 cargo] military plane. Just simply ducking, running and carrying children. We simply laid the babies on the floor of the aircraft and sat next to them and cared for them."

The first orphan plane crashed on takeoff, killing 154 of 330 people on board. It was a mechanical failure, but the pilot of the plane carrying the Kights' children didn't know that. To avoid ground fire, the plane took off at a steep angle, causing the children to tumble toward the tail. "Some were pretty banged up," said Kight.

All of the children had adoptive parents waiting. Kight's job was to receive, feed and care for them until they could be matched with their new families. She had three days to prepare. Calculating that the house could accommodate forty-six children, Kight called an emergency meeting at Concord. Could the members feed, bathe and care for the twenty oldest children at the 1724 meetinghouse?

"We leveled with them," she recalled. "We said, 'You are not getting little sweetie pies. These kids are from a war-torn county. They don't speak the language and some of them have seen their parents shot before their eyes.'" Oh, and two other things: Kight didn't know how long the job would last and she wouldn't be available to help.

The Quakers looked at each other. Sure, they said.

A Catholic seminary supplied mattresses. Volunteers organized themselves into teams to staff both sites 24/7. When Grace told her Drexel classes that she wouldn't be there for their last two meetings and final exam, more than fifty students volunteered. Books were stripped from the study so that diapers, towels and clothing could be stacked on the shelves. Furniture went to the neighbors. Toys and play equipment appeared. Stan checked into the Media Inn.

Spooked by the orphans' backgrounds, some adoptive parents backed out. Some worried that the children were diseased. But other parents stepped forward, including several volunteers. Barbara French, who worked at Kight's house and now lives in Florida, made Tran Van Minh, age eight and half African American, her fourth child. As an adult, Marty Van French served as a navy navigator in Iraq.

"This job was not done by anyone alone," said Kight. "The volunteers all handled the kids very carefully. And they all hunted me up at the end of each day to say, 'Thanks for letting me take part in this terrific thing.'"

How many other Nam vets say that?

READING LIST

Brown, John K. *The Baldwin Locomotive Works*. Baltimore, MD: Johns Hopkins University Press, 2001.

Brown, Kenneth A. *Inventors at Work*. Redmond, WA: Microsoft Press, 1988.

Carter, W. Hodding. *Flushed: How the Plumber Saved Civilization*. New York: Atria Publishing, 2007.

Chernow, Ron. *House of Morgan*. New York: Atlantic Books, 2003.

Clark, Cherie. *After Sorrow Comes Joy*. Westminster, CO: Lawrence & Thomas Publishing House, 2001.

Clayton, Thomas Jefferson. *Rambles and Reflections*. Chester, PA: Press of the Delaware County Republican, 1892.

Dawson, Jim. *Rock Around the Clock*. San Francisco, CA: Backbeat Books, 2005.

Dell, Roberta E. *United States against Bergdoll: How the Government Spent Twenty Years and Millions of Dollars to Capture and Punish America's Most Notorious Draft Dodger*. New York: A.S. Barnes & Co., 1977.

Fones-Wolf, Ken. "Mass Strikes, Corporate Strategies." *Pennsylvania Magazine of History and Biography* 110, Historical Society of Pennsylvania (1986): 447–57.

Frady, Marshall. *Martin Luther King, Jr.: A Life*. New York: Penguin, 2005.

Haley, John W., and John Von Hoelle. *Sound and Glory: The Incredible Story of Bill Haley, the Father of Rock 'N' Roll and the Music That Shook the World*. Wilmington, DE: Dyne-Amer Publications, 1991.

Howe, Neil, and William Strauss. *Generations: The History of America's Future, 1584 to 2069*. New York: Harpers, 1991.

Ogle, Maureen. *All the Modern Conveniences*. Baltimore, MD: Johns Hopkins University Press, 2000.

Roberts, Randy. *Jack Dempsey, the Manassa Mauler*. Champaign, IL: University of Illinois Press, 2003.

Sharpless, Isaac. *A Quaker Experiment in Government: History of Quaker Government in Pennsylvania, 1682–1783*. Philadelphia: Ferris & Leach, 1902.

Shaw, Anna Howard. *Story of a Pioneer*. New York: Harper & Brothers Publishers, 1929.

Spector, Robert. *Shared Values: A History of Kimberly-Clark*. Lyme, CT: Greenwich Publishing Group, 1997.

Surowiecki, James. "Turn of the Century." *Wired*, January 2002.

Taylor, Bayard. *The Story of Kennett*. New York: G.P. Putnam & Sons, 1866.

Thomas, Hugh. *The Slave Trade: The Story of the Atlantic Slave Trade, 1440–1870*. New York: Simon & Schuster, 1999.

Warden, Rosemary S. "The Infamous Fitch: The Tory Bandit James Fitzpatrick of Chester County." *Pennsylvania History* 62, no. 3 (1995): 376–87.

About the Author

M ark E. Dixon has lived in the Delaware Valley since 1987, when he moved from Texas to a Drexel Hill apartment complex where *American Bandstand*'s Dick Clark once lived. Though not himself a native, he grew up hearing about "the beautiful city of Philadelphia" from his mother, who moved here in 1945 to do social work and ended up marrying a Hahnemann University medical student from Michigan. And the roots go deeper: Dixon's mother chose Philadelphia based on stories told by *her* grandmother. In 1886, Dixon's great-grandmother—a descendant of some of the region's earliest settlers—was a shopgirl at Wanamaker's Grand Court, opposite city hall in Philadelphia. And there, though it was surely against John Wanamaker's rules, great-grandmother let herself be romanced by—and later married—a midwestern Quaker who was in town on business but needing

a pair of gloves. Those tales provided a window into the area's history, later supplemented by Dixon's joining the Religious Society of Friends (Quakers)—which, he observes, is practically a historical society itself.

The public relations job that drew Dixon to the area vanished in a spectacular corporate bankruptcy three years later. Eventually, he returned to work as a writer—this time, freelance—building on earlier experience as a reporter for newspapers and trade publications. The stories in this book are columns that he began writing for *Main Line Today* magazine in 2003. Dixon and his family live in Wayne.